Life Among the Poor in Cairo

Unni Wikan

LIFE AMONG THE POOR IN CAIRO

Translated by
Ann Henning

TAVISTOCK PUBLICATIONS

First published as *Fattigfolk i Cairo* by
Gyldendal Norsk Forlag, Oslo, in 1976

This English translation first published in 1980 by
Tavistock Publications Ltd
11 New Fetter Lane, London EC4P 4EE

Published in the USA by
Tavistock Publications
in association with Methuen, Inc.
733 Third Avenue, New York, NY 10017

© 1980 Unni Wikan

Typeset by Red Lion Setters, London
Printed in Great Britain at
the University Press, Cambridge

All rights reserved. No part of this book
may be reprinted or reproduced or utilized
in any form or by any electronic,
mechanical, or other means, now known or
hereinafter invented, including
photocopying and recording, or in any
information storage or retrieval system,
without permission in writing from the
publishers.

British Library Cataloguing in Publication Data
Wikan, Unni
   Life among the poor in Cairo
   1. Women – Egypt – Cairo – Social conditions
   2. Cairo – Poor
   I. Title
   301.41'2'096216   HQ1793   80-40091

ISBN 0-422-76970-3
ISBN 0-422-76980-0 Pbk

Contents

Acknowledgements vi
Preface vii
Foreword by Nils Christie viii
1 Field work among the poor of Cairo 1
2 The back streets as a place to live 16
3 What is poverty? 26
4 Main features of the social system of the back streets 41
5 Some of the children's social experiences whilst growing up 64
6 Intrigue-spinning and the forming of alliances surrounding betrothal 81
7 Role formation within marriage 96
8 Self-realization in a poor environment 123
9 Possibilities of change in living conditions 148
 Appendix – prices 168
 Bibliography 169

Acknowledgements

I would like to thank a number of people without whose help and encouragement this book could not have been written. First of all, Fredrik Barth my husband; Laila Shukry el Hamamsy, the dynamic leader of The Social Research Center; and the late Chris Thoron, formerly President of the American University, who were constant sources of moral and practical support while my field work was in progress. Peter Anker, former Norwegian Ambassador to Cairo, was my guarantor in various ministries, and it may well have been due to his prestige and influence that my work could take place at all. Vivi Täckholm was a tremendous source of inspiration and provided me with a much appreciated refuge during the last stage of my field work. Moreover, she contributed sacks full of clothes for my poor friends. Nils and Vigdis Christie, Harald Tambs-Lyche, and Albert Henrik Mohn gave me much-needed encouragement to write this book, and useful comments on the first synopsis. Lillan Steen has also read the script and given me much good advice, and Eli Langmyhr has been a patient typist. Inger-Lise and Knut Mørkved, and Frøydis and Roger Johannessen gave me support and friendship when I needed it most during my field work in Cairo. I also want to express my heartfelt thanks to the Norwegian Research Council for Science and the Humanities for the necessary financial backing.

Oslo, 2 May 1975   *Unni Wikan*

Preface

This book was written with the sole aim of creating understanding and respect for the people it describes. In no way do I intend to blame them for their behaviour patterns or attitudes. I see them as the unfortunate victims of a situation from which it is incredibly difficult to emerge. At the same time, I hope that the understanding of the life of the poor in Cairo will involve the reader more deeply in the social and human problems which afflict many of the poor people living in the world. My book contains a harsh description of the living conditions and the environment of the poor in Cairo, but this should not be seen as a criticism of the Egyptian authorities, who cannot be blamed for the country's lack of resources and its development problems. I sincerely hope that the reader will come to share the warmth and sympathy I myself feel towards the people I describe in the book. In order to protect their anonymity, I have chosen photographs which illustrate the environment without identifying the people in question.

Foreword

by Nils Christie

This is an important book. It goes straight to the heart of the matter; straight to the matter of poverty, describing the effect of extreme material deprivation on interhuman relations.

A respected wife in Cairo receives gifts from her husband. This is a pleasant custom which favours family relationships, provided gifts *can* be bought. If a wife does not receive any gifts, she is degraded. Poor men are thus forced by social conditions to degrade their wives. If the wife does not even receive the minimum amount of money needed for rent and food for the children, she is even further degraded. Wives who are constantly degraded are not easy to live with — and so the men spend most of their time away from the apparent symbol of their own insufficiency. The women and children are left alone in the back streets, where their state of poverty erodes any form of alternative social relations. Women are sometimes able to try to support or at least comfort each other, but they do this only in very small and unstable circles, limited as they are by poverty. Women-friends are expected to compensate them for everything they lack. The women have no possessions, so they establish relationships in which they praise each other for having at least moral assets. But women can only trust each other if they have *complete* loyalty. This makes it impossible to have more than one woman-friend, since every conflict demands a taking of sides. The environment is conspicuous for a huge number of alliances — and counter-alliances. The degradation of others becomes a way to upgrade oneself. This makes for a hard and vindictive environment. Even from the social point of view, being poor is expensive.

This study describes women's experiences of poverty. At the same time it complements other studies of the effects of poverty.

A remarkable likeness exists between in particular the poor

people of Cairo and the slum populations of the USA. Elliot Liebow, in *Tallys Corner, A Study of Negro Streetcorner Men* (1967) has described men in the slums of Washington as 'fathers without children'. They are too poor – and too insecure – to dare to assume normal family obligations – or to maintain them, if they dare assume them. Unni Wikan describes mothers forced to act almost as if they were men. In both cases people are forced into situations by material deprivation. In both cases it is obvious that these material conditions must be changed for the systems to work. Not until then will people be able to realize the ideals set by themselves for a life of dignity.

Seen from the outside, both men and women often behave in an irrational and repulsive manner. Unni Wikan gives many examples of this and also describes her own despair and reluctance at the beginning of the field work. But I notice that most of her reluctance gradually disappears as she manages to get inside the system. After finishing the book, one is left with a basic feeling of despair about the problems the poor of Cairo are facing, together with respect for the good qualities they have managed to keep in this situation of extreme deprivation.

ONE
Field work among the poor in Cairo

This book tells the story of life in a poor quarter of Cairo as it is experienced by the poor people themselves. It also seeks to analyse the circumstances which bring about this life situation, and in this analysis I choose as my point of departure the poor people's own understanding of their life situation.

The field work on which this book is based was done over eight months: September-December 1969, November-January 1970-71, and August 1972. I began the work after having already spent two years in Egypt. One of those years I spent doing an intensive course in Arabic at the American University in Cairo. This enabled me to work without an interpreter, and to use the method which in social anthropology is often called participant observation. Social anthropology is the comparative study of societies and cultures, and the most adequate data are obtained through participation in the life of the community which is being studied. Whereas an interviewer with a questionnaire merely seeks answers to questions which have already been formulated from an outside point of view, the anthropologist tries through participation to learn to think as people do themselves, and to experience the same conditions as those under which *they* live. Thus, she makes friends. She tries to take part in all manner of daily activities. She endeavours to behave 'properly' from the point of view of the people in that particular culture, thereby affecting minimally the flow of life which she observes. At the same time, she cuts herself off from her former life. Consequently the people in the foreign culture become overwhelmingly important to her, because they are, in fact, her only, or at best her main human contact, and so she becomes especially sensitive to their reactions and opinions. In this manner, the anthropologist places herself in a uniquely intensive learning situation, in which it becomes possible to a large extent to assimilate a foreign culture. This, however, is a process which takes a long time.

Without financial support it would have been impossible for me to carry out this study, and I would therefore like to extend heartfelt thanks to The Social Research Centre at the American University in Cairo who financed most of my work, and to the Norwegian Research Council for Science and the Humanities and The Norwegian Foreign Office for travel grants. I would also like to thank the Egyptian Government, which generously offered me grants via the Ministry for Higher Education.

Access to the back-street environment was obtained through a friend of a friend who had an uncle in this area. I got to know Hassan's family, where Umm Ali[1] is the housewife. Hassan was then a forty-three-year-old mechanic. Umm Ali was thirty-three, and the couple had six children between the ages of two and eighteen. The family is slightly better off than others by local standards. I told them I was interested in practising colloquial Arabic, but that this was impossible at the American University where people 'are so pretentious they only speak English or French'. I also wanted to learn more about the customs and manners of poor Egyptians, I said, explaining that I studied sociology (*il'ilm iligtimā'i*) since in Arabic there is no word for anthropology. At this time I was afraid to emphasize my interest in the social sciences too much. Egyptians are well known for their suspicion of each other and of strangers. The Egyptian anthropologist Hamed Ammar, for example, says in his book *Growing Up in an Egyptian Village* that he was totally unable to obtain usable stories about people's lives — in spite of the fact that he was studying the village where he himself had been born and had grown up. The villagers were afraid of saying things which could be considered slanderous, especially when their testimony was taken down and thus could reach official circles. They took the attitude that personal conditions should be concealed and protected, not revealed to outsiders. This is confirmed by an interesting linguistic phenomenon: if you ask how they are, people often reply that the condition is undisclosed, not revealed, not open to others (*mastūr ilhāl*), that is: 'We're fine.' The American sociologist Morroe Berger met with the same problem when he designed a questionnaire directed to higher Egyptian officials. In a letter explaining the character and intentions of his design, he tried to

---

[1] 'Umm Ali' means Ali's mother. After having their first child, women are renamed 'the mother of —'.

encourage the interviewees to co-operate by stressing the fact that the answers would be strictly confidential, and that he was not interested in their 'opinions' about things, only in 'certain personal data'. In Western sociology, such an approach has proved effective. When he showed the draft letter to some of his Egyptian assistants, however, they could not even begin to understand his implicit reasoning. It then turned out that the Egyptians' view was the complete opposite of Berger's regarding the way to *encourage* civil servants to co-operate. According to the judgements of the Egyptians it would be totally devastating to ask for 'personal data', whereas 'opinions' were quite harmless.

I began my field work fully prepared to come across problems like these in gaining the confidence of the poor, and thus in assessing the trustworthiness of my information. I was also aware of the widespread fear of espionage in the country at the time, only a year after the Six Day War. I therefore chose to 'dissimulate': I never told my poor friends – with one exception – what role they and their private lives would play as material for my book. It can be said against me that I took advantage of the trust of my friends and deceived them. However, I hope that the people described in this book will not feel that they have been used, so long as the information provided cannot possibly harm them. And I do not believe it can since it is not accessible to relatives, neighbours, or friends, i.e. the people they fear might hurt them. On the contrary, I hope that it may become a positive – although modest – contribution to helping the poor people of this world, including my friends in Cairo. The purpose of my work – apart from giving a close anthropological description of the lives of poor people in Cairo – is to try to contribute in two ways to improving their conditions. First, I want to open the eyes of as many readers as possible to the humiliating human conditions created by poverty; to show how poverty pervades and vulgarizes all aspects of life, debases social relations, and cripples individual potential for development and happiness. It is my hope that increased knowledge and understanding will lead to greater sympathy, and at best, to a greater will to help actively. I also hope that by showing concretely *how* poverty has these tragic consequences, I will direct people's compassion towards the areas where their desire to give effective help can be most useful.

As I mentioned above, there was only one person among the poor people in whom I dared confide the real purpose of my field work. This woman was Umm Ali. She accepted and supported my intentions. She promptly invited me to live with her family and suggested that we protect ourselves against any gossip (see p. 48) by saying that I had come with greetings to the family from a distant relative in Paris.

I could not possibly have had a better starting-point than Hassan's family. Umm Ali is an exceptionally wise, tolerant, and warm-hearted person, with perceptive understanding of herself and her society. She was very open with me, and confided in me her thoughts and emotions. By so doing, she gave me an intimate understanding of the world of a poor, married woman, and throughout my field work she remained my most important source of insight. Thanks to her I could quickly establish deeper and more genuine friendships with other, less open women. On the whole, I could say that my friendship with Umm Ali, both for this work and for me personally, has been invaluable.

The perspective of this book is thus in essence the women's perspective — the poor quarter seen through the eyes of the poor woman. And so it had to be, since sexual segregation on this level of Egyptian society is so strict that I was severely restricted in my interaction with the men. Besides, it is characteristic of participant observation as methodology that one's understanding is always coloured by the particular viewpoint one assumes, although one gains insight into society as a whole. In this society I was prevented from assuming the point of view of the men, but it is the women's perspective as I obtained it which gives the deepest insight into family life and community among the poor.

I immediately accepted Umm Ali's offer to stay with her family, and moved in with them. But their living conditions proved too hard for me. I had to share one wide single bed with two plump teenage girls. I lay in the middle, the bed was full of fleas, and I itched like mad whilst being almost unable to move, squashed as I was between my two bedmates. We slept seven people in a small room three metres square, with a temperature of 30°C (86°F) and no ventilation. In this way the nights became a strain rather than a rest and I became unable to face a new day with energy and enthusiasm. It was also difficult to get enough to eat, but that was my own fault. The poor families competed among themselves to get me to eat with them. But naturally, poor people in Cairo do not have the same views on hygiene as we do. Ideas about what is acceptable and what is not acceptable vary greatly from one culture to another. Intellectually, I completely accepted the poor people's standards; and I knew that if I had been born into their world I would have shared their values. But I had problems emotionally. I was so disgusted by the way they treated their food, that I ate very little, and only in order not to insult them. It was common to see cockroaches, pigeons, and rabbits eating the bread that was being served (pets often eat bread here), and it was not uncommon for the children to relieve themselves on the floor, and for the bread to fall into their excrement, whereupon the adults happily put the same precious piece of bread into their mouths. Such events, which dramatically demonstrated the difference between my hygienic standards and theirs, gave me a general feeling of revulsion against all their food. They would have felt the same revulsion if I had offered them pork – a Moslem could not possibly think of a more impure kind of food.

It became increasingly difficult for me to share completely the living conditions of the poor. After three to four weeks in Umm Ali's house I capitulated and moved into my own flat, which I had to find outside the poor quarter since any adult woman living there alone would be considered a prostitute. Nevertheless, I was afraid in the beginning that I might never manage to complete my work, simply due to the fact that I might not be able to put up with the filth and stench which permeate this environment. But it is incredible what one can get used to. Now, when I go back to see them, I hardly see the filth nor notice the stench.

Through Umm Ali I got to know many neighbours and relatives. Neither Umm Ali nor I needed to take any initiative. At the moment when the incredible news spread that a foreigner (*xawàga*) had moved in with Umm Ali, people came swarming from all directions to see the phenomenon. I was stared at for hours, and became irritated, hurt, and annoyed by this avidity and by the complete lack of tact. But since I was unsure of myself and did not want to risk ruining any contacts by an insult, I dared not object. I got my own back later, however, when I felt more confident and had learnt what forms of expression are allowed in this culture. 'What do you think I am, a movie?' I shrieked – and they immediately left me alone.

Everyone who came to see me at Umm Ali's insisted that I come and see them. The minute they had left, Umm Ali advised me against taking them up on it. 'Only evil comes from mixing with people – nobody here wishes anybody else well.' Two exceptions, she said, were her two friends, I could safely go and see them. I was irritated by her exaggerated suspicion, as I saw it, and by her attempts to monopolize me. But since I was dependent on her, I did not dare ignore her advice. At first, therefore, I contacted women of whom she either approved or at least did not directly disapprove. They were very few. But as I began to feel more secure in my friendship with her, I dared make contact with more women – who all gave me the same advice: 'Don't go to such and such. Nothing good will come of it ...', etc. When I ignored these warnings, I was duly punished. Women who had met me trustingly became suspicious and estranged themselves from me. Only Umm Ali was tolerant enough not to let herself be put off. It was obvious that my attempts to see several women and have them all as 'equally good friends' was simply not acceptable. The reason was quite clear: they had never in their lives seen or heard of a woman who went from door to door being friendly with everyone. In their world, such behaviour was not only absurd, it was inconceivable. The demands and the risks entailed in friendship were so extensive, and the suspicion against people in general was so strong, that no one ever had more than two to three friends. Many had just one.

For a little while I did not know what to do. How could I possibly learn about the lives of poor people in Cairo if I only knew three to four families? But then I had an idea: to use my identity as a Christian. This notion came to me after hearing how they constantly pointed out differences between Moslems and Christians: 'You Christians love your fellow beings. You have compassion and solidarity. We Moslems do not have good hearts. Nobody wishes anybody well.' By referring to my identity as a Christian, I could make them accept, and even understand to a certain extent, that I had many friends – including some who were enemies.

Figure 1

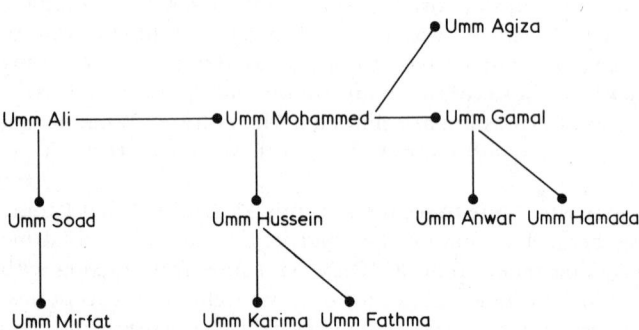

This, however, did not solve the whole problem. For next they wanted to know who was my very *best* friend. 'Whom do you like most, me or her, us or them?' they would ask me. It was no use to try

Figure 2

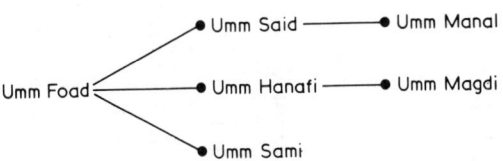

and dismiss the question by saying that I liked them all equally well, or to swear to each one separately that I prefererred her/them. For they had their own way of measuring love: frequency and duration of visits. To love equally meant visiting each woman equally often and for an equally long time. And thus began a real farce. They tried to compel me to show my love by *demanding* that I visit them and by keeping me with them by force once I had come. I tried to protect my freedom to choose for myself whom I wanted to visit and for how long. They put enormous pressure on me by constant cross-examinations to find out where I had been and whom I had seen. I countered by trying to spread my contacts in the area, so that it became possible for me to visit some without necessarily being observed by the others. But then they sent their children along to find out, if they suspected I was anywhere near. When I continued to ignore their demands, some of them threatened to break off our friendship. 'We won't be friends with you any more' – and to refuse to let me visit them again. At first I took such threats seriously. When I finally lost my temper and challenged them: 'O.K., so I don't care if I'm friends with you or not! Goodbye; and peace be upon you then,' they came rushing after me full of repentance. In due course they developed a standard excuse for my strange behaviour: 'Leave her alone. You know she loves everybody .'

Through all these difficulties a group of seventeen families was crystallized with whom I developed stable, friendly relations. The key persons and the ways I came into touch with them are shown in *Figures 1* and *2*. The network of relations which connects many of these families is shown in *Figure 3*. The seventeen families were not a random sample, in the sociological sense of the word, but I have tried to make sure that they are representative for the range of differences in poverty and stage of family development found in the area, and I would claim that they are all typical of the poor people in Cairo.

As a participant observer, the anthropologist is dependent upon

8 *Life Among the Poor in Cairo*

Figure 3

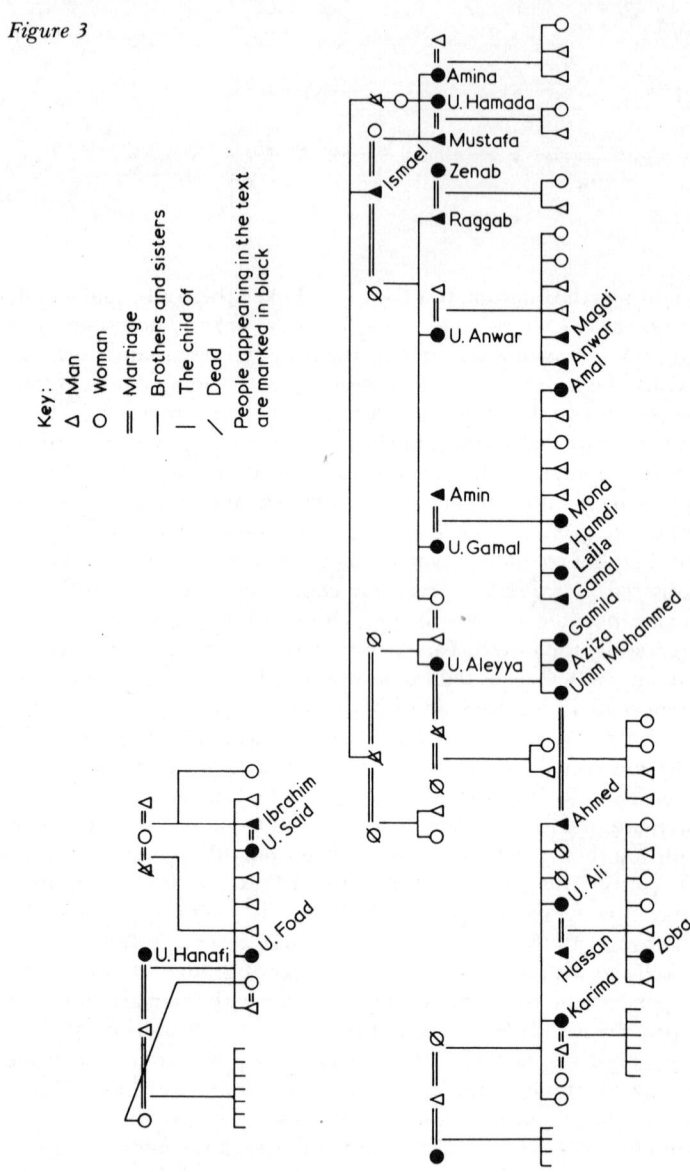

the people of the foreign culture as her sole, or at least her main, source of human contact. Consequently, it is extremely important to her that the temperaments of these people – their emotional tenor and their style – harmonize with her own. This will affect whether she feels at ease and the extent to which she will be able to develop an empathy and understanding for the foreign society. I was very lucky in this respect. I felt I could grasp intuitively both the vulnerability, the jealousy, and the suspicion of the poor, and also their extrovert qualities, their naivity and warmth. Meanwhile, I felt I could express genuine traits of my own character in a way that they could accept. The fact that people *express* their feelings was quite natural to them, and therefore they would accept emotional outbursts from me even when they did not understand the reason behind them. When we were together they readily revealed their happiness and grief, and even when they tried to be tactful and polite, they were unsubtle enough to enable me easily to understand what they really felt. It was not until later during fieldwork among Arabs in Oman in 1974, that I fully appreciated how much all this actually meant for my work. The contrast between the Egyptians and the Omanis is as great as that between Italians and Englishmen. The Omanis always show genuine tact, courtesy, and respect to all people. Even a stranger is treated as a true fellow-human. But the self-discipline they thereby assume becomes so strong that they are difficult to reach emotionally. I seldom knew what they really felt or thought, and could never see through the facade. And what was equally difficult, I never felt that I could be myself with them. I always had to be controlled, courteous, and respectful to accommodate to their norms. It was an exasperating experience and also very unsatisfactory. How I longed to be back with my friends in Cairo! The contrast with Oman also made me appreciate another aspect of life among the poor: it was never dull. Whereas I became quite desperate living the monotonous, eventless life of Oman, the field work in Cairo exhausted me by its constant dramatic events. As we anthropologists look back upon completed fieldwork, we easily come to romanticize our field experiences, and beautify the now distant people and conditions. To make sure that I am not giving such an idealized picture here, I would like to quote from my field notes:

Monday, August 7, 1972. My God, I'm sick and tired of this life. Quarrels *everywhere*, gossip and slander, hypocrisy and self-praise – the stench, the piss and filth and garbage, kids fighting and screaming voices penetrating absolutely everywhere.

Life Among the Poor in Cairo

Figure 4

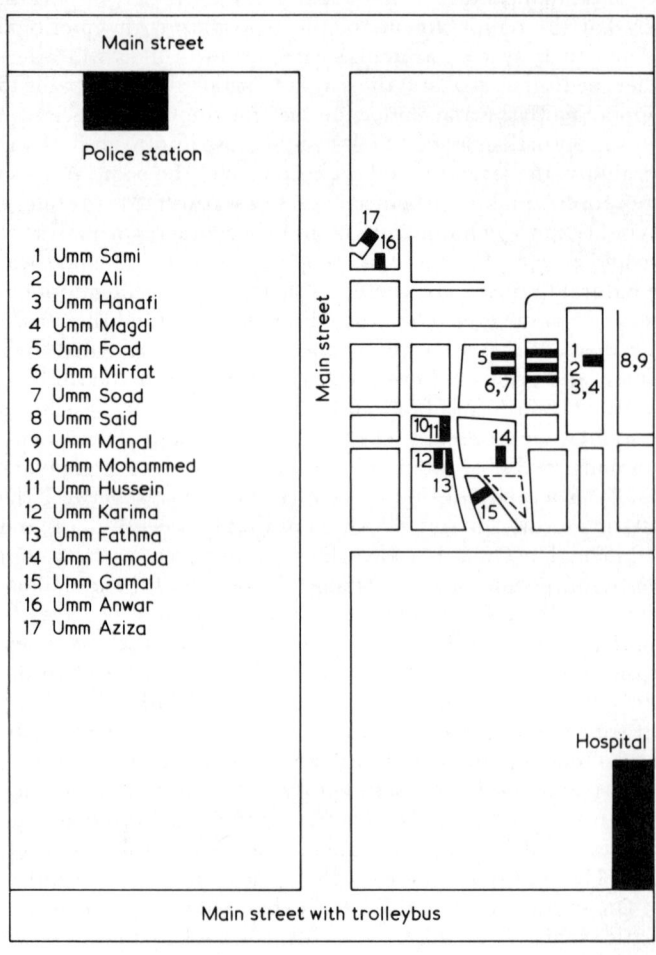

Obviously it's really getting on my nerves now, because I feel the stench is in my clothes and in my hair, and I'm sure the caretaker at my hotel can *smell* what kind of area I've been to. Many memories/images are disgusting to me now because I'm tired and dislike them: Umm Ali's Nora who pees and does everything on her mother's lap – she gets the kids to wipe it off with a cloth, but she doesn't change her skirt for hours. Today Nora defecated on the floor, and they just wiped it with a piece of paper. Umm Zenab turned the cushion on the divan and then said it was Fahima's boy – that is, not the daughter's child! – who had peed on it; the sight of quarrelsome and unkempt women and their voices, shrill and vulgar, their nerves on edge, making them scream and row and fight for the slightest thing, adults and kids helter-skelter: 'You bitch, you daughter of a whore, you cow, you whore, I'll kill you!' etc. – a revolting smell of cooking everywhere, for example today when Umm Abdullah got up and shook out her apron – the stench was like a cloud around her. And then the stench from the lavatory filling the kitchen, especially when the wind blows in that direction. In the street they shout and scream, there are quarrels and rows, morning, day and night. I don't think I've spent one single evening in this area without seeing a quarrel involving a physical fight, women and men together. And then the hypocrisy, for example Karima praying: 'See how religious I am', she seems to be saying. She's in the middle of her prayer when her son comes in and I wait anxiously to see what will happen. And just as I expected, her curiosity and bitterness get the better of her, the prayer is forgotten and the quarrel begins . . .

There were also other aspects of my work situation in the field which created difficulties. Since I lived in an apartment outside the area, I had to get in every morning and out every night, except for some special occasions when I spent the night there. Then I had to travel on overfull buses where most of the passengers were men, and most of them tried to fondle me. But once I arrived at the bus stop by the poor neighbourhood the worst trial awaited me: to get into the area I had to run the gauntlet of the market street which was very crowded and included a large number of men who were a constant annoyance. I developed a defence technique, hitting my handbag against any man who came near me, and also acquired the greatest repertoire of invective in the area. It helped, but not enough to stop me dreading the trip each day. I did not know anyone in the streets I had to pass through, and as a result I was often bombarded with garbage, and naturally with foul names. But it was not so strange, after all. People must have been wondering what I was doing there, perhaps they thought I was a spy. So they threw rotten tomatoes and oranges and potatoes and stones – and dirty water from the higher floors. But I was never hurt, and most of the time I think my tormentors were children who wanted to show off.

Living outside the area also entailed difficulties when it came to taking notes: I had to wait until evening before I could take down any information. And once evening came, I was often so exhausted that I waited until the next evening and the next . . . I dared not take notes while I was there, due to people's suspicions and their possible fear of me being a spy. After some time, however, I developed a technique by which I took down the key words as guidance, pretending they were new Arabic words I was learning. But this could only be done in situations which permitted such interruptions on my side.

Still, there was one great advantage in living outside the poor quarter: the freedom to allocate my time as I saw fit. If I had lived within the area I would have been exposed to visitors at all times of day and night, and I would have been worn out by constant socializing all round the clock. In participant observation, the anthropologist tries to place herself in the same situation as the people whose life she is trying to understand. By virtue of this, she inevitably develops personal close relationships to people in the community and identifies strongly with them. At the same time she knows that she really belongs to a different world, and is sharing these living conditions only temporarily, and to a limited extent. In the course of my field work, this progressively developed into a painful and haunting awareness that my situation was really very different from that of the poor. I had, for example, privileges and influence which could have been of great value to the poor, if I had made them available. It became *too* painful for me to be only a passive spectator of all their suffering and need, and I felt I had to do *something* for them. But my attempts made me realise how very difficult it can be to do good, even with the best intentions. Our actions in a strange environment often have consequences which we cannot possibly foresee.

My initiative was released by Ramadan in 1969. Custom demands that the children dress up in fine new clothes for the celebration at the end of the month. This symbolizes that a new year has begun, unblemished by the enmities and sins of the last year. The clothes become a condition of taking part in the celebrations; without them they will be scorned by the other children. As the feast approached, I witnessed so many tears and quarrels that I decided to help on a large scale. I made a collection of unwanted clothes among all the Norwegian women living in Cairo, and the Norwegian Embassy cooperated by sending a car round to collect the clothes. The result was far beyond my expectations. Literally a whole room in the Embassy was filled, from the floor almost to the ceiling, with all sorts of clothes, hundreds of pairs of shoes, etc. This then had to be distributed. The Norwegian Embassy generously offered to lend two men to pack the gifts and a car to take the gifts into the poor quarter. But I was afraid the car might be badly damaged by people who would probably crowd up and become uncontrollable at the sight of such riches within reach. Moreover, I was not quite sure how many gifts we should prepare. I had not considered the criteria for allotment: need, friendly relations with me, locality, merit? Would they feel shame at receiving gifts? I came to the conclusion that the best thing would be to distribute the clothes separately and secretly to the families I knew.

The distribution took some time. Every day for nearly a month I struggled under the weight of fully-loaded sacks, in order to share everything out in time for the festivities. To the best of my ability I tried to distribute the clothes as justly as possible. And the effect of my 'charity' was devastating: a little joy – but mostly an avalanche of jealousy, slander, and rows among the recipients. With a single exception, everyone was dissatisfied with what they received. Everyone wanted the best clothes, and they were all afraid or sure that I gave more and better things to others than to them. Typically, no one wanted to share with anyone, except possibly poor people outside the area, that is, people who were not their rivals. In their efforts to stop me from giving to others they beseiged me with evil slander about how undeserving all others were: 'You can go and see for yourself – they have cupboards *full* of clothes!' I was plied with the most unbelievable stories about how wealthy everybody else was, even those who were the most obviously impoverished: 'You can't see it, you see, because they *eat* up their money!' Even sisters who had so far stressed what an exceptionally good relationship they had, abandoned all resolutions and slandered each other. Some even approached me with direct demands and begging, such as Umm Karima who, with tears in her eyes, showed me a washed-out, tattered dress, saying in a broken voice that she had had to beg it from a friend for her daughter, and imploring me to give her something better for the celebration the following day. But when morning came, the daughter appeared in a lovely, newly-made dress – which she certainly had not got from me! People who had so far been kindly disposed but who did not know me and consequently could not reach me with either slander, begging, or demands, became hostile and spiteful when they saw me pass. They stood by, silently approving as the children bombarded me with stones and potatoes. Between the recipients of the charity, rivalry became so strong that new enmities exploded and old ones were rekindled. Overnight the whole neighbourhood seemed to have been transformed into a witches' cauldron where the only things people wanted to talk about were the evils and wrongdoings and revenges of years past.

How could it all go so wrong when I tried so hard to make the distribution as just as possible? A good deal of the explanation lies precisely in my own idea of justice: I thought people should receive help in proportion to their objective needs, regardless of my private sympathies or antipathies. Consequently it became in their own interest to show themselves as poor and needy as possible. When the lies became *too* apparent, they tried eliminating rivals by arguing that they were so vulgar and slovenly that they would not look after whatever they might get in any case. But equally important was the fact that they simply could not accept my *impersonal* ideal of justice. They thought I ought to give the best and the most to those I liked best, regardless of that person's financial position. They saw the gifts as an expression of love, of the quality of my relationship with them. To them friendship is an obligation which *cannot* be cast aside. Thus, to try to treat friends in the same way as other people, following objective rules for justice, was to them a denial of the friendship. Therefore they felt I let them down as a friend and reacted accordingly. I on my side was hurt and disappointed by what I only saw as greed and heartlessness towards people who might be just as deprived as themselves. I did not understand that to them there *was* no conflict between their need for the clothes and their desire for proof of my friendship. Neither did I realize how difficult it must be for them to accept impersonal, objective justice from me, when they live in a world where personal relations determine whatever they attain: work, pension, flat, hospital beds. . . . My reactions, in other words, were determined by my specific, Norwegian ideas, and not by consideration of the recipients' reaction to my charity. Thus my 'charity' became an arbitrary exercise of power, in which I forced the consequences of *my* ideas on to the poor. I was in a privileged position, having access to these riches, and I could do as I wished.

Could this have been done differently, and in a way which might have spared the families this storm of envy and discord? Many readers may argue that the best solution would have been to let the people of the neighbourhood form a committee for the distribution — thereby leaving the decisions as to who should have what with the poor, who had their own ideas of justice and merit. But I am sure that such a committee would have created even worse havoc than I did. I believe that the committee members would have started fighting physically about which of *them* should have the most and best – and no one else would have seen any of the clothes! (see p. 135).

The only practicable solution that I have been able to think of is one I have practised on similar occasions later: I have given things mainly to the people who are close to me, and I have made each family come and collect its share directly from me – in that way it is not obvious to the neighbours that I am bringing clothes to the house.

My attempts to practise charity serve as an illustration of how complex a society is, how intricately its aspects are interconnected, and how actions at one point may have consequences and secondary effects far beyond what one might expect. To achieve even the simplest and best intentions, one needs to command an understanding of these interconnections within society, or else one might find that one is doing ill in the name of charity.

TWO
The back streets as a place to live

About two-thirds of the six million inhabitants of Cairo live in areas which both Egyptians and we would characterize as poor quarters. This is an analysis of the life situation of seventeen families living in one such quarter.

The families live in thirteen houses situated in five back streets. All these houses are less than three to four minutes' walk apart, and some are only a stone's throw from each other. Some of the seventeen families are interrelated, some do not know each other, not even by name; some are more or less acquainted and say hello when they meet, or drop by to see each other occasionally; some are intimate friends, others are self-confessed enemies, not on speaking terms. Indirectly, however, they are all connected in a network of social relations (see the Introduction) and they share the same life situation.

The back streets housing the seventeen families are not part of a neighbourhood with a name or definite boundaries, either physical or social. Therefore, the neighbourhood is not a ghetto in the sense in which the word has been used for American slums. The population is not culturally distinctive (i.e. an identifiable minority), or class homogenous. Neither is the area segregated by categorical social barriers. Among the poor, there are different degrees of poverty – differences which have certain consequences for interpersonal relations, as we will see below. Some of them are Coptic Christians, but most are Moslems. All of them, however, think of themselves nationally as Egyptians, and they all speak the same language. Two of the seventeen families are Coptic, but there is little in their life style to separate them from the Moslems. Administratively, the area belongs to Giza (Gozen in the Bible), which is one of the thirteen large districts of Cairo. This unit has a name, official institutions, and defined borders. In 1961, the population of this district amounted to about 300,000. The total population of Cairo was then 3.4 million people. Since then, the total population of Cairo has risen to six million, and I presume that the population increase in the district has been even higher in proportion. It has probably more than doubled, since the poorer neighbourhoods, here as in other large cities of the world, have a much sharper rise in population than the upper- or middle-class neighbourhoods.

The district has been populated since time immemorial, and has long been classified as one of Cairo's poor quarters. Today, however, it also includes some good, modern areas, even some beautiful upper-class neighbourhoods. A factor analysis carried out by Janet Abu-Lughod (1972) of the thirteen districts in Cairo also places this neighbourhood in the lowest socio-economic category as a slum.

The district is divided into main streets and back streets (*shāriça* and *ḥāra*). The main streets are the official traffic routes, and the only parts of the area of which the better-off inhabitants of Cairo, or foreigners, may ever catch a glimpse as they pass *through* the district. For such people would never stop there — the clamour in the streets, the stench, and the noise clearly announce that this place is only to be visited or inhabited by the very poor.

Nevertheless, the main streets are 'a nice area' to the really poor, compared to their own back streets. They are at least three times wider (often much more), and far cleaner, with larger houses and far better maintained facades. Back street people call them 'French neighbourhood' (*ḥitta frangi*) as opposed to the 'folk' neighbourhood (*ḥitta baladi*) where they live themselves. (*Baladi* connotes simple, coarse, traditional, undeveloped, etc.). The dichotomy stands for an important contrast of life styles, which they think represents the two different kinds of neighbourhood (whether their observation is empirically confirmed or not is irrelevant in this context). People living in French neighbourhoods are educated, they stay indoors, and do not poke their noses into their neighbours' affairs. 'No one sits by the door with hawk's eyes watching to see what the neighbour's husband brings back for supper', is the common expression of the poor. Neither do they hang out of their windows hurling abuse at each other, nor attack each other in the street. 'Each person keeps to himself' (*Kulli wāḥid fi ḥālu*), as people should, in direct contrast to the blameworthy conditions of their own neighbourhood.

The back streets as a place to live

Physically and socially, the back streets form a characteristic environment. The streets themselves are like alleys, often no more than 2.5-3 metres wide. They are floating in refuse and filth, often stinking so badly that the stench hits you as you turn round a street corner – this despite the fact that the dustman comes to clean every day.

Along both sides, there are houses standing wall to wall from 5-6 to 9-10 per block. They are built of brick, and are mostly three storeys high with two flats per floor, but some have four storeys, and some have only one flat per floor. The same front door and stairs are used by all the people living in one house; that is, between twenty-five and forty adults and children.

Most houses are also back to back with others which have their front doors facing the next parallel little street. In most cases, there is no backyard to separate the two rows of houses, but in some places there may be a shaft about 1.5 metres square where the drains from the lavatories are. This is then used as a chicken or pigeon yard by the people living on the ground floor. An indication of the crowded conditions is the fact that the chickens, pigeons, ducks, and rabbits which most families breed, usually have to be kept on the balconies or stairs, or in the lavatories. Sheep may also be kept in the flats, but this happens less often. One of my better-off families has two sheep tethered in the kitchen.

The flats are built in such a way that each has one or two small windows facing the street. Several flats on the first, second, and third floors also have a balcony. People live so close to each other that neighbours can easily look straight into the flat opposite if the curtains are open – which they have to be to let in both light and air. But that way they may also let in the neighbours' curious glances which they would certainly much rather do without. This lack of privacy creates friction which will occasionally explode in angry confrontations, when the parties involved hurl abuse at each other from their windows while the rest of the street forms an interested and appreciative audience. The person who stares, however, always has right on his or her side, for according to public opinion, everybody can behave as they like (that is, sit staring out of the window) inside their own flat. (*Ilwáḥid ḥurr fi shaqqitu* – everyone is autonomous in their flat.)

The street is the scene of many different social activities. Men are conspicuous by their absence, as they spend both their working and leisure hours away from the neighbourhood. The leading actors are therefore women and children. The streets are swarming with children playing, screaming, and shouting; barelegged and thinly dressed all year round. Outside many front doors are women sitting or standing, observing the life unfolding in front of them. They are old or young, stand alone or two or three together, dressed in black, long-sleeved, almost full-length dresses, or patterned habits which look rather like nightdresses. No one is veiled. Most of those dressed in black are older women. Some of them are sitting comfortably on a stone outside their front door, where they prefer to spend a great deal or most of the day. The others speak contemptuously of them as 'door-sitters'.

Other women, younger or older, only come out occasionally to look for their children, to catch a breath of fresh air, or, in winter, to warm themselves in the sun. The younger ones very often carry an infant in their arms. They have a chat with the neighbours with whom they are on friendly terms, or with the 'door-sitters' (*illi biyuqçudu'āla ilbibān*) if they are friends. Other women pass on different errands, alone or a couple together, the younger ones often with a child or two tagging along. They are practically all women from the neighbourhood, that is, the closest surrounding streets, and strangers are extremely rare. The passers-by stop and talk for a while if they meet friends on the way, utter a word or two to acquaintances, and fleetingly greet or ignore the rest of the people they pass; that is, most of them.

People also take part in the life of the streets from balconies and windows, as either actors or audience. Well-trained and discriminating eyes closely observe anyone who comes or goes, taking in what they wear from top to toe, what they carry, who they are with: all this is socially important information. Sudden bursts of conflict are watched and commented upon. There is hardly a day without vehement confrontations for one reason or other, when the combatants bring out their whole overwhelming repertoire of abuse and threaten to attack each other physically, which often happens. Scenes where women tear at each other's hair or bodices, grab pebbles, rotten tomatoes, potatoes, dirty water, or old shoes to use as missiles, or wooden planks as swords; or where men draw knives against each other, are a common part of life in the back streets.

Accommodation

The houses are privately owned, and both men and women own them. Most house owners have one, some just a half, and very few two to three. None of my seventeen families own houses. One man – the wealthiest amongst the people in my study – once owned half a house but had to sell it due to quarrels between his wife and his sister, who owned the other half. Many of the house owners live in the back streets in their own houses; the others come at the beginning of the month to collect the rent. The rent is established once and for all when the rental agreement is entered into – it is prohibited by law to change the terms after that. The flat is let unfurnished and the house owner is under no obligation to maintain it. The only service he must supply is water, but he evades this obligation as far as possible by having a water tank supplying the whole house or even two houses next to each other, if he owns them both. The result is a constant water shortage on the first, second, and third floors. The people living on these floors often have to carry water from the ground floor when the people there are washing their clothes. The size and standard of the flats vary. On some of the rooftops there are temporary wooden shacks, put up to serve as accommodation for the poorest of the poor. Other people have only an earth-floored basement room at their disposal, often without a window, and share sink and lavatory with others in the entrance hall. Both these arrangements are called 'rooms' (óḍa) by the poor, whereas a flat (shaqqa) consists of at least two rooms. Of my seventeen families one lives in a wooden shack, three in basement rooms, and the rest in flats.

Although the flats are all different, they have certain common features. The rooms are small and dark, and cockroaches, bedbugs, beetles, and other vermin thrive. The walls are of plaster but full of cracks and holes, since not even new plaster is very durable. The floor is stone. All flats have running cold water, none have hot water. The kitchen is usually a tiny nook with a bench, pots and tubs, and one or two gas rings. It is always next door to the lavatory, and the door to the lavatory is usually in the kitchen. As a result, the kitchen is the one place in the flat which is really pervaded by the stench from the lavatory. The lavatory itself is a room of about 1 metre square with a hole in the floor for waste, a water tap, and a shower on the wall. There is no ventilation, and it is a favourite haunt of cockroaches.

The flats are overcrowded. It is difficult to find an accurate measure of the degree of overcrowding in these flats. None of the indices developed by social scientists (e.g. A.L. Shorr (1970)) of number of people per room, number of m^2 per person, and a separation of activities in different rooms (such as separate bedrooms and sitting-rooms) seem to me adequate. Amongst my seventeen families I found a variation of 1.2-4.5 persons per room in the flats, and 1.2-5 m² per person. The families living in wooden shacks on the roof, however, had only 0.4 m² of floor space and 0.3 m² of roof per person. The separation of activities in different rooms was in all cases very incomplete: one cooks, eats, sleeps, sits and sees visitors, and has the children do their homework, in the same room.

Such statistics, however, do not take into account differences between cultures in what is regarded as elementary needs. In some places, people *wish* to be close together and to carry on all sorts of activities in the same room. Therefore, I find it more adequate to measure overcrowding in terms of the degree to which the tenants themselves feel that they fail to fulfil some of their cherished values because of lack of space.

Some of these values are: (1) Everyone should be able to sleep in a bed. This is regarded as absolutely necessary in winter, when the stone floor becomes icy cold. (2) The parents and children of more than four years of age should sleep in separate rooms. (3) Brothers and sisters from puberty on should sleep in separate rooms. (4) Unrelated male guests should be received in a room which does not serve as a bedroom or sitting-room for women. (5) Each family should have a kitchen which is protected from curious, critical visitors (see p. 145).

In terms of this the seventeen families score as follows:

(1) No family has beds for all family members. By bed I mean one divan, one single bed, or half a double bed. It is an established value among the poor that nubile young girls and married women should be fat. In general, therefore, women are grossly overweight and consequently need a lot of bed-space. A summary of the number of people and the number of beds in the seventeen families shows that 100 people between them have fifty-seven beds at their disposal. The table is shown below.

Table 2(1): *Available beds*

	Number per family	
adults	1 3 3 2 2 3 2 3 2 3 2 3 5 3 2 2 1	
teenagers	1 2 2 2 3 3 1	= 100 persons
children	1 5 3 4 4 2 3 3 4 2 3 3 3 2 2	
beds	0 2 4 4 4 4 3 2 4½ 6 3 4 4 7 2 2 1½	= 57 beds

The remaining sixteen families put several persons together in the beds to avoid having to use the floor. To let up to *seven* children or teenagers sleep in a large bed is a feasible solution. I also know of three families where the floor is used regularly for sleeping. (2) Of the fourteen complete families, only one has enough space to allow the parents and children over four years of age to sleep in separate rooms. (3) Four of the families have teenagers of opposite sex. They all sleep in the same room. (4) Six families have a 'drawing-room' (*odit gulus*) for visitors. But it is important here to note that five of these six families are at an early stage of development: the couples have been married for less than ten years and have no more than three children. As the family grows, the furniture often has to be sold and exchanged for beds, and the 'drawing-room' becomes a bedroom or sitting-room. The one family at a later stage of development which has a 'drawing-room' only achieves this by letting almost half of the eleven family members sleep on the floor in the other rooms of the flat. (5) Six families do not have a kitchen.

Some general differences between the flats seem to be due to their situation, whether they are on the ground floor or higher up. The ground floor flats are the darkest of all, because the street is so narrow that it excludes the light. In addition, the walls are thickest on the ground floor, and the windows are deep, excluding sunshine completely. These flats are moreover damper and colder than the other flats. The floor is of earth or stone laid directly on the ground. No breath of air ever finds its way in; the floor and walls can never be aired, and dampness clings to them. In winter, when the night temperature falls to 5°C (41°F), the dampness can be so appalling that the icy cold stone walls emit a rotten stench and the people living there have to keep the primus burning all night to keep warm.

In summer these flats are the most agreeable as long as the sun is up, when the average day temperature in Cairo approaches 40°C (105°F). But the problem of airing remains, and the heat and the dampness absorbed by the walls during the day makes the air in the rooms intensely hot and stifling during the night. Sometimes people get so desperate that they go out and sleep in the street at night. During the day, they choose to leave open the door to the stairs, to the annoyance of the tenants who then have to pass it.

There are further problems for those who live on the ground floor. Cockroaches and other vermin are more troublesome here, and the stench from the lavatory is more annoying, because ground floor tenants are closer to the common drains from all the lavatories of the house. They also find it difficult to dry their washing, since they have no balcony and therefore are dependent on other people's good will. And one ambition which some people in the poor quarter try hard to realize, which is to stop the children playing in the street, becomes more difficult the closer the front door is to the street. The children *want* to go out; the street is their playground, indeed the only spacious place they have. My data, and other impressions of life in the back streets, indicate that there is a connection between living on the ground floor and sitting by the door, the diagnostic feature of 'the folk neighbourhood'. 'Door-sitting' (see p.19) is seen as a vulgar and low habit because it is wrong for women to sit outside staring – they should stay indoors, minding their own business. The behaviour of the 'door-sitters' consequently indicates to all those who do not sit by their doors that this person has different moral values. However, I do not share this view. I have noticed that the 'door-sitters' are women from the darkest, smallest, lowest flats, that is, women with a good reason to want to leave their rooms, which are even worse than the average. I see their behaviour as an adjustment to particularly bad accommodation, not as an indication that they consider 'door-sitting' right and proper, nor that they are more interested than others in 'what the neighbour's husband brings back for supper' as their non-door-sitting neighbours maintain. (Hannerz (1970) speaks generally about this tendency among all people to draw conclusions about other people's values from their behaviour.)

The fact that the flats on the ground floor are generally of a worse standard than the others does not mean that the better-off among the poor never live there. Some flats on the ground floor are of a better standard than some of the flats higher up. Or the tenants may prefer a ground floor flat because they have lived there for a long time, the rent is low, and they feel attached to it, and/or they are elderly and want to avoid stairs. The housing shortage in Cairo is another factor. These days it costs a lot in key money to get a new flat.

Mobility

Settlement in the neighbourhood is relatively stable. Most of the inhabitants of the back streets have lived there since starting their families. But there is some movement and circulation among the population. Rooms and flats are evacuated for various reasons, usually enmity between neighbours, quarrels between house owners and tenants, or changes of marital status, such as divorce or death. People already living in the neighbourhood often have friends they would like to have near, and some new neighbours are recruited in that way. Others are found by flat agencies. My material shows the following pattern.

At the beginning of my first field work period in September 1969, fourteen out of the seventeen families were complete family units, that is, they consisted of mother, father, and children. Out of the fourteen heads of the families, ten had grown up within walking distance (i.e. a maximum of 15-20 minutes) of their present home. Eight out of the seventeen women had grown up there, and nine had moved in from other poor neighbourhoods in Cairo. On 1 August, 1972, only one family unit had been dissolved. If we relate the remaining thirteen complete families' duration of tenancy in their present flat to the duration of their last marriage, it turns out that nine families had lived in the same flat since they got married. Among the others, two had left flats which were within walking distance of their present accommodation. Both moved because they had quarrelled with neighbours. The other two came from other parts of Cairo, but both had relatives in this neighbourhood and wanted to live closer to them. Three out of the seventeen families were incomplete when my field work started. In two cases this was due to death, and in one to divorce. Another couple divorced before I finished the field work. In all these cases, the change of marital status resulted in a change of abode for the parties involved.

Let me now summarize those features of the life situation in the back streets which I judge to have the most important implications for the kind of life people here can create. It follows from the picture I have drawn that the focus must be on constraints and limitations on life, rather than opportunities for fulfilment. Indeed, this perspective also coincides with the way in which the poor people themselves experience their environment.

The neighbourhood *is* a *ḥitta baladi* – a simple neighbourhood – and felt to be a compromising place to live by most of those residing there. It becomes very important for anyone with pretensions to try to disassociate themselves from this environment. One lives in overcrowded flats and with the neighbours very close. Anyone who comes and goes and whatever they carry or bring, is avidly observed by dozens of door-sitters, window-peepers, and balcony-standers. Much of what happens inside the flats behind closed doors, is also overheard by neighbours, since noisy quarrelling is a characteristic part of life here. In other words, a 'back-stage' – a protected place where people can let down their defences – hardly exists.[1] And yet, neighbours are so disloyal and alienated that a thief can walk in during the middle of the day and walk off with objects as large as radios, and the neighbours will not intervene.

Relations with the big city

The back streets do not form a closed world to the people who live there. They are clearly dependent on places and institutions, partly in the main streets nearby, partly in other parts of Cairo. This is most obvious when it comes to work. The breadwinners in my sample worked in many different parts of Cairo. Only three of the working people had their main job within walking distance of home. Most depend on long bus journeys. Schools, hospitals, doctors, offices, post offices and telegraph stations, police stations and similar offices and institutions on which the population depend are within walking distance of the five little streets. The law courts, on the other hand, where most heads of families have appeared at least once, can only be reached by bus. Moreover, the population do most of their shopping for food, clothes, and household things in the nearest main street. The women go there every day when they have money to buy food for dinner. In the back streets there are only a few rickety sheds, stocked with a selection of goods which satisfy the immediate needs for cheaper things. In the main street there are also services of different kinds for the back-street people: barbers, shoemakers, furniture repairers, etc., while men ironing clothes, and tailors and seamstresses operate in the back streets.

Finally, it should be noted that the back-street people are not only forced out of the poor neighbourhood by their dependence, physically and socially, on the larger milieu around them; they also *seek* to go out, by their own choice, for instance to visit friends and relatives in other parts of Cairo.

---

[1] Social life is often compared to the theatre: we act out roles which we want a larger audience to see, but behind the scenes – 'backstage' – we prepare our appearances and relax in protected, isolated surroundings (See Goffman, *The Presentation of Self in Everyday Life*).

THREE
What is poverty?

I have emphasized the fact that this is a *poor* population, which gives rise to the question: what is poverty? Is it possible to give a universal, cross-cultural definition of this phenomenon? Social scientists have tried, applying different criteria. Some assume that there are certain universal, human, biological needs which can be specified, and if these are not adequately satisfied – people may be defined as 'poor' (e.g. A.L. Shorr 1970). As far as I know, however, it is only with respect to nutrition and accommodation that work has been done aiming to establish such standards (M. Rein 1970). But even if it should prove possible to identify these standards, I think that 'biological needs' are quite unsatisfactory as a measure of poverty. People may both eat and live in a physiologically adequate manner but still see themselves, and be seen by others, as poor. And then they *are* poor – in the social sense of the word.

The starting-point for any analysis of poverty must consequently be how people themselves experience their own life situation, and whether this is confirmed by others. The category 'poor' is created through interaction, and has social reality, I would argue, only to the extent that the parties to the interaction agree on the criteria which define the categorization.

In other words, it is a necessary condition for poverty that there are real differences in material standards within the population. Stone-age people were not poor, because there were no better-off people with whom they could compare themselves. Consequently, they could not experience their situation as one of deprivation. But differences alone are not sufficient to create a category of poor people. People can try to conceal their deprivation, and it is only when this is revealed that they will be seen by others as poor. Even then they may not necessarily end up in the category of poor people. An Indian ascetic, for example, chooses deliberately to go through life renouncing material goods. He himself considers his life-style to be the most praiseworthy and his fellow men admire and revere him. A gipsy's lifestyle, on the other hand, is seen by many sedentary people as disgraceful and far from praiseworthy, but if the gypsies themselves have a system of values which praises this style, they are not poor in their own eyes. Therefore, it is only in cases where the better-off and worse-off agree on a low evaluation, and the deprivation is transformed into social defeat and disgrace, that the real situation of poverty arises.

This is the situation of the poor in Cairo. They have no special and distinctive system of values of their own to protect them. Their culture, their values, and their attitudes are on the whole the same as those of the surrounding city. They agree about the disgrace associated with the kind of life they lead – they feel inferior and degraded as persons because of the way they are forced to live. Their lives become an endless sequence of testimonies, from others as well as from themselves, to their failure. The evidence springs from many sources: life at home with constant conflicts due to lack of money; the neighbourhood where small differences in material standard are seized upon as differences of human value. 'I'm better than you! I eat, drink and dress better than you!' *(ana aḥsan minnik, bakul, bashrab, balbis aḥsan minnik!)* is a typical taunt during confrontations. The people living in the main streets are different from the back-street people and are, by comparison, *better* people. Each bus trip goes through areas with even better houses and private villas, among people driving around in private cars, whilst they are catching their breath in the second class compartment of an overfull bus, or even hanging on to the outside of the bus to avoid paying the penny for the ticket; past restaurants where they will never set foot, and past crowds of people who are obviously much better off than they are. Every encounter with bureaucracy emphatically stamps them as insignificant, such encounters being determined above all by the social status of the client as assessed from his clothing. They are seen as poor nobodies who cannot bribe or threaten, and are treated accordingly. On radio and TV there are plays about successful people. There are 'those who are cultivated' *(izzawāt)* and 'those who are poor' *(ilfuqara)*, cultural categories which rank whole persons and govern interaction. The Koran and Hadith sayings of the Prophet provide authoritative standards of behaviour which the poor are prevented from fulfilling by sheer lack of money. And many of the cultural values essential for

Egyptian identity, such as hospitality, they are condemned to practise only as verbal ideals (see pp. 132-3).

Poverty, consequently, is created only within a stratified system where the different groups have similar or shared standards of evaluation for the essential material preconditions for a dignified human life. Moreover, poverty is a condition which afflicts the whole person. Deprivation pervades life. It influences the activities of the poor person in all his roles. Poverty, in its implications, thus resembles the concept of impurity which creates differences between castes. But unlike caste status, it is difficult to describe poverty in *positive* terms — it is *what they lack* which characterizes the poor. In order to characterize poverty positively, one can only say with Walter (1966) that it implies 'plenty of what nobody wants'.

Such, then, is the life situation of the seventeen families. They can all be defined as typical representatives of a poor population. Let me begin my documentation by looking at their sources of income and its distribution. Almost all of these families have only one working member. Among the fourteen complete families, the wife has her own income in only one case. Some have a teenage son or daughter who goes to work and spends the money they earn on clothes for themselves. But the general statement stands: only one member of the family is the provider and responsible for the economy of the household.

The level of pay is affected by the fact that the employees sell unskilled labour. Only four out of the seventeen providers have the equivalent of O-levels, and most of them have not completed elementary schooling. They have learned their jobs as apprentices. Most of them (eleven men) are employed in the public sector. Their jobs have the advantage that they can only be dismissed if they have committed a crime. The others work for various small private companies and must take care that they do not lose their jobs in this country of widespread unemployment.

Table 3(1) below identifies the jobs, and the incomes derived from the employees' main jobs. The level of pay varies primarily in proportion to the length of employment. In public companies wages go up by about £0.75 monthly, in private ones by a little less. The net monthly wages of the men vary from £7 to £51. The fixed income for most is, however, about £10-£16 a month. (1972 figures.)

This information has been obtained from the poor themselves, in most cases, from women. It is possible that the figures in some cases are £1-£2 too low, from an attempt to elicit money from the anthropologist. The distortion can, however, not be too great, because wages are fairly standardized, and I have therefore in most cases been able to confirm the information.

The working hours in the main jobs are between six and eight hours daily. Most employees finish work at 3.00 to 4.00 p.m. and thus have most of the afternoon and all evening free. They also have one whole day off per week. Under the pressure of poverty almost all employees in the sample choose to use much of this spare time earning a secondary income, the possibilities being working overtime or doing various kinds of little jobs: one clerk makes rose water and sells it to grocers, another works as a plumber, professional drivers drive taxis, etc. Where overtime is concerned, the country introduced a law in 1969 giving priority to people on a fixed salary of less than £40 per month. With this extra work, most of the employees in my sample work on average as many as ten hours per day.

Table 3(1) specifies the types of extra jobs taken by the providers in the seventeen households. As can be seen, only three have chosen not to have any extra income. One of these sees it, however, as an investment in a higher income in the long term, as he is attending evening classes to take the equivalent of A-levels. This is possible only because he lives in his father's flat and pays no rent, but this arrangement is fraught with conflict. The other two are the very poorest in my sample — one lives in a miserable wooden shack on an earth roof, and the other in a basement room without a window, with an earth floor. The situation of both is, however, such that extra work is impossible: one is constantly ill with rheumatism, and the other is a widow who can only hold down her first job by leaving her seven-year-old daughter alone and unattended until five o'clock in the afternoon, while she herself works. To leave the girl to look after herself after dark as well would be unthinkable. Because these two are caught in a miserable economy, and have no chance to do extra work, both are forced to compensate with measures which are culturally especially degrading: the husband sends his wife out washing when there is a chance, and the widow has had to send out a nine-year-old child to work for strangers, in order to have one mouth less to feed.

Table 3(1) gives only approximate and incomplete details about the size of the secondary incomes. There are two reasons for this: (1) The incomes vary, and are difficult to specify. They are obtained irregularly and in small instalments so the provider himself does not necessarily know what they are. (2) All the men's

Table 3(1): Sources of income per household[6]

head of family	composition			main job	extra job	main income £	extra income £	total £
	adults	teenagers	children					
mother	1	1x	1	washer-woman		3	4[1]	7
mother	3xxx						4[2]	4
father	2	4	1	mechanic	overtime	10	4	14
father	2		3	clerk	plumber	10	5	15
father	2		4	bank-clerk	overtime	12	3	15
father	3x	2	4	clerk	juice prod.	16	7	23
father	2		2	tailor	overtime	9	2	11
father	3x	2	4	baker		8	4.50[3]	12.50
father	2		4	driver	taxi driver	14	14	28[4]
father	2		3	driver	taxi driver	12	8	20
father	5xxx	3x	3		pension	51	0	51
father	3	2x	3	caretaker asst.	barber	16	?	25?
father	3xx	3	3	mechanic		18	?	30?
father	2		2	mechanic		8	0	8
father	2		2	electrician	overtime	9	3	12
father	2		2	electrician	overtime	10	?	16?
mother	2	1	2				9[5]	9

x) one person supports himself with extra income
1) widow's pension
2) the woman receives £4 from three adult sons together
3) the main provider receives £2 from his son with an extra job and £2.50 from the husband of a daughter living at home, separated; during the main provider's frequent illnesses, his wife works as a washerwoman.
4) the provider has to pay his father's family £2.50 per month
5) this household consists of mother and two daughters working as apprentice seamstresses; this extra income represents the total contributions from mother's brothers and the daughters' half-brother on the father's side and the daughters' earnings as apprentices
6) this household table was made at a different time to the table showing beds (see p. 0)

private expenses for cigarettes, coffee, and transport are covered by their secondary incomes, whilst only some of it, or none, goes to the household. The men consequently find it important to hide the amounts from their wives, as an expression of their independence and autonomy.

Attempts to keep the amounts secret in order to reduce or eliminate demands from people with financial claims on them (including their wives) are common, and can be done most effectively with the secondary income. During all my interactions with men, women were always present and the information given to me by the men about secondary incomes is therefore unreliable. For most providers I have only been able to make estimates regarding the amount, based on what I know about the pay levels of different types of jobs and the approximate number of hours the men invest in these jobs.

It seems to me that the total monthly wages of the twelve providers with secondary incomes must be £11-£30. I suppose that most of them earn less than £20, whereas very few make as much as £30 and this only by working as hard as they possibly can as a last resort to satisfy the particularly pressing needs of a large family.

How much a monthly salary of £8-£30 represents as material resources to a family can only be evaluated in relation to the expenses it has to cover. My source of information is again statements by the families themselves, as well as observations of consumption patterns and price levels.

None of the seventeen families keeps any kind of account of the running expenses. Only one has an account with the grocer with her expenses specified in figures rather than goods, and this system is seen as particularly disgraceful. The details about different expenses were given primarily by women, since shopping and household economy are their duties. When it comes to fixed monthly expenses, they only know the amounts for two to three stipulated items: rent, co-operative ration of tea, sugar, rice, and cooking oil, and electricity, if they have it. Some know how much money they allot each month to the different items, since the husband gives them a fixed sum for these purposes, but sometimes he may give a little extra. Others do not know, because their husbands give them a little housekeeping money from day to day, perhaps even divided into morning, day, and night, according to what he has. Sometimes he will bring back food after having left the family without food in the morning. At other times they go without food. In other words, most families are unable to budget and plan and they see their financial situation as chaotic.

With these reservations I can give the figures for the following monthly expenses. The rent varies from £1 for a basement room with earth floor to £3-£5 for a flat with two to three rooms. The amount depends on the situation of the flat and how long the tenant has had it. The electricity bill for a flat with two to three rooms is between £0.75 and £2.00. The other expenses naturally vary in proportion to the number of family members. The fourteen complete families, nine of which are at an early stage of development (i.e. the wife is only about twenty-five years old) have an average of 4.4 children. Let us look first at a typical family (i.e. four children) and calculate its monthly expenses where they are specifiable.

	£
rent	2.50-5.00
co-op ration	0.75
electricity	1.00
soap	1.75
paraffin	0.75
total	6.75-9.25

Other fixed monthly expenses include food and the husband's personal expenses (including his travel to work). Where food is concerned, my families seem to agree that 40-50p daily is good and sufficient for a family of six. This means a monthly expense of £12-£15. None of my families consume anything like this. But let me show how much the ideal amount would represent in buying power, by giving the price levels of the desired goods, and thus show how modest their dreams of satisfaction actually are. The figures are from the summer of 1972, and give the price per kilogram if not otherwise specified: meat 75p, fish 18-30p, rice 5p, macaroni 7p, potatoes 2p, vegetables 2-5p[1], milk 10p, eggs 1p each, cooking oil 20p, sugar 15p[2], margarine 25p, butter 70-90p. Bread is 1p for a white loaf (*çesh frangi* = French bread), 0.5p for the traditional brown bread (*çesh baladi* = the simple people's bread).

With these price levels the families have to make do with a diet consisting almost exclusively of rice, bread, and vegetables, with tea as the daily, almost the only, drink. One must bear in mind the fact that the men with their demanding jobs need a reasonable number of calories per day and also that women, in order to realize the

[1] In winter the price doubles.
[2] Most households must supplement the co-op ration.

cultural ideal of obesity, eat disproportionately large amounts. On the few occasions when these people taste meat – it can be from once a week to once a month – the meal consists mainly of rice, tomatoes, and bread with only two to three tiny, precious pieces of meat per person. They are obsessed with their diet themselves, and fantasies and dreams about food are ever-recurring topics of conversation. They express a clear understanding of the need for nutritious food (*çesa*) which they define as meat, fish, eggs, milk, and cheese. They blame malnutrition as the main reason for their physical and mental fatigue.

I hoped to be able to estimate how much a family actually spends on food by asking two women with families of identical size and composition to give me lists of the dishes they usually make for dinner. The lists were almost identical. On the basis of them I could calculate that a family needs 5p per person per day if they are to eat enough to feel full. This means expenses for food of 30p per day or £9 per month for the sample family of six members. It was obvious that none of my families had such amounts at their disposal, and that the exercise had failed to give the desired result – a measurement of actual consumption – since the women, quite naturally, did not list their improvised solutions in emergency situations.

The amount the husband spends privately I can only guess, using my knowledge of the price of cigarettes, travel, and tea at the cafés. It seems to me that 20p per day would be a possible average. The few men who do not smoke spend much less, for a packet of twenty cigarettes is about 12p.

These calculations give £24 as the fixed monthly expenses for a family of six, provided they eat sufficient quantities of their most common types of food. On top of this comes a long series of irregular but essential and inevitable expenses which have to be covered: clothes, household utensils (including linen, towels, etc.) medical care, school fees, ritual celebrations, etc. The price levels of these are given in the Appendix.

On the basis of these data, it should be obvious that all the seventeen families live in a chronic financial crisis judged by culturally acknowledged standards for material consumption. Some of the families always tend to have more to spend than others, but all have periods which are even more desperate than average. But the situation for all of them has the same fundamental character, and the people are forced to juggle constantly with their all too scant resources to cover many essential and competing expenses. The problem is most acutely experienced by the woman. Her task is to allocate the limited resources. She is at home all day long; she is the one who has to handle the problems of expenses, and sees them as critical. Her husband is out for most of the day, and his concerns centre on the difficulties of making rather than allocating. How this is reflected in the conflicts and reciprocal roles of spouses is my theme in Chapter 7. Here I am trying to establish the fundamental discrepancy between income and expectations from life which drives everyone to use a series of emergency solutions in a situation which is basically insoluble.

The standard solutions applied by the families are:

(1) *To reduce the outlay for food.* This is the simplest and most common saving a woman can make. One possibility is to eat rice only, and/or beans with bread. It also happens now and then that people go without food for a day.

(2) *Consumption and payments are postponed for as long as possible.* They do not go to see a doctor until the pain becomes unbearable and they often put away prescriptions for a year or so, because the patient or his provider finds the expense too great. School-children have to manage with four note books instead of the ten the teacher demands. It is common to owe rent for one or two months. Around Ramadan it is a rule and not an exception that people owe rent for three months; that is, the festive month itself and the months immediately before and after. Even at other times people may use this solution for a period of three to seven months. This, however, can easily lead to sanctions from the house owner. I happen to know that four of the families have been in court because they owed rent for three to six months. A fifth returned home one day to find that the door of her flat had been broken up and all her furniture, a bed and a cupboard, had been thrown out into the street. Two legs of the cupboard were broken and the bedclothes had fallen into the dirt of the street. The culprit was the house owner and the reason the fact that the tenant owed him rent for two months.

(3) *Money is borrowed.* Women keep turning to this solution to cover acute minor expenditure. The amounts may be from 5p to £1. They borrow from male relatives or close women-friends. The men are firmly against this practice and would only use it themselves as a way out of 'great problems', as they themselves see it. In such cases they prefer to borrow from work-mates. Numerous conflicts between spouses arise from the wife's borrowing, and this reflects their respective sensitivity to complications connected with either making the money or making it last. Borrowing money to a woman means a temporary solution to an overwhelming problem,

but to a man it is no solution at all, since he has to make that extra bit of money in turn. Besides, it is disgraceful to the husband to reveal that he cannot keep his family.

(4) *Belongings are sold.* All the wives in the study have sold the golden bracelets, the earrings, and the ring which they were given as a betrothal or wedding gift from the husband, in accordance with tradition. Slightly used clothes and shoes, kitchen utensils, even beds and cupboards are also sold in emergencies to friends. On one occasion a man gave his glasses to a friend to whom he owed money. The friend then came to me to find out how much he could get for them.

(5) *The cheapest kind of goods are bought*, although numerous experiences show that cheap goods prove expensive in the long run. The women, for example, constantly feel miserable physically because, they say, they use the cheapest type of contraceptive pill. The 'good type', which they believe contain vitamins, cost 15p more, and are therefore beyond their reach (see p. 158).

(6) *Hire purchase is practised to a large extent*, for clothes, linen, and furniture. The item is paid for over four to five months and becomes about 25 per cent more expensive.

(7) *Saving clubs (gam çiyya) are established* by an initiator (*ra'is*) and recruitment is based on friendship relations. Mutual trust among the members is necessary. The women have their clubs among the neighbours and the men theirs at their work or more commonly, they join the neighbourhood club through their wives. The members pay a regular contribution (per day, week, or month). Each time they pay, a premium is paid to one member, amounting to 30p to £50 per member. People can, however, join with a half, one, or several memberships. The initiator gets the first premium, and then the turn for payments is determined by negotiations or lottery when the club is established. If the payments to the club are not made, the initiator is responsible to the other members and may have to – by informal sanctions – sell her personal belongings. Conflicts are very common, partly for this reason but also because the members maintain that the initiator does not follow the verbally agreed list of payment priority. The initiator can use the saving club as a means of covering any unexpectedly large expenses. For the members, the club is the only possible form of saving they can practise in a situation of deprivation where they find it impossible to put money aside in the house and *not* use it to meet acute needs for food and clothes. Therefore most women are at all times members of one or more saving clubs. (I do not have the equivalent data about the men.)

(8) *Occasions calling for material expenditure are avoided.* On ritual occasions such as childbirth, circumcision, and the feast accompanying Ramadan most people who, according to cultural tradition, ought to bring little gifts, fail to appear. They fail to go and offer their condolences because the custom demands black shoes, which they do not possess. Sometimes a quarrel is provoked to create a situation where one is not on speaking terms with a person who could make material demands (see p. 107). This then makes it impossible for them to demand anything. They refuse to accept hospitality to ensure that they will not have to pay it back. Even when a family chooses to invest its scant resources in expensive private education (see p. 155) they often keep the children at home for the first month, hoping to avoid paying the £3 (i.e. between a third and a quarter of the yearly school fee) which is collected during this month. The month of Ramadan is the most conflict-ridden in the whole year, just because it demands great expenditure which simply cannot be evaded.

(9) *The wife seeks employment* as a maid, washerwoman, or factory worker, but this solution is seen as the last resort. Many men say they would rather jump into the Nile than be publicly disgraced like that.

The point is that these solutions do not represent alternatives among which people can choose in order to solve a specific problem. Most of them are actual features of people's lives at any one moment; strategies which may well be practised concurrently.

I shall illustrate this with four examples of the financial position (income and outgoings) at a point in time chosen at random. I suggest that the examples are representative of the slum households.

Example 1: A family of two adults and three small children.

Fixed outgoings for August 1972:

	£
rent	5.00
saving club	1.00
electricity	0.60
co-operation	0.50
payment on carpet	1.00
payment on sheets	0.50
	8.60
Total fixed income	15.00

less fixed outgoings	8.60
sum remaining for food, clothing, and all other needs	6.40

Example 2: A family of two adults and three small children. The provider has financial obligations to his father and sister.

Fixed outgoings for August 1972:

	£
rent	4.00
electricity	1.00
co-operation	0.50
soap	2.00
to father	2.00
to sister	3.20
	12.70
total fixed income	14.00
less fixed outgoings	12.70
sum remaining for food, clothing, and all other needs	1.30

Example 3: A family of two adults and three small children. The provider gets his first wages in three months, having been without a fixed job for two months. Whilst he was unemployed, he borrowed 20p per day from his mother to keep his family, and he had some extra income as a cab driver.

Fixed outgoings for November 1969:

	£
two months' rent	7.00
debt to husband's mother	13.00
debt to friend	2.00
co-operation for two months	1.00
festive clothes for seven-year-old son	6.00
	29.00
total fixed income	20.00
saving club	6.00
total income	26.00

less fixed outgoings	29.00
remainder	−3.00

Example 4: Family of two adults and seven children.

Financial position in August 1972:

	£
fixed income	15.70
less two deductions on bank loan	3.00
deduction on special loan for clothes	2.25
net fixed income	10.45

Husband and wife have an agreement that the wife has a right to £12 a month for housekeeping money. The husband pays the rent of £2.20 out of his extra income from rosewater production which amounts to about £7 per month. At the end of August the family owes rent for three months, i.e. £6.60. The provider does not expect to be able to pay rent until he has paid off his bank loans, i.e. in another six months.[1]

The wife buys most foodstuffs, soap, and paraffin on account from the grocer's and pays at the end of each month.

The previous month the bill from the grocer amounted to £10.50. Due to illness the wife could only pay £9. At the end of this month the family will therefore owe the grocer for goods in August approximately £10.50, plus debt from July, £1.50.

The family's financial position in August is as follows:

	£
net fixed income:	10.45
secondary income:	7.00
total income:	17.45
Necessary outlay:	
debt to grocer	12.00
rent	6.60

---

[1] This loan is given to public employees in connection with Ramadan, payable over eight months. In 1972, August will be the last month, and the family will then have a net income of £12.70.

other foodstuffs	?
transport, cigarettes, coffee	?
clothes, medical care	?
necessary outlay	£18.60 + ?

It is apparent that at the end of this month the family will be even deeper in debt. On 17 August the family had, moreover, already spent £7.25 at the grocer's. The husband was furious, and the wife cried desperately in fear that the account at the end of this month would be even higher than £10.50.

These data substantiate my claim that we are dealing with poor families. I have shown what the situation of poverty implies in terms of material income relative to minimum needs, as Egyptian culture defines them. The following chapters will show how all social life is affected by the material deprivation, both by the objective limitations it imposes on the individual's life and by the cultural and social patterns it creates.

FOUR
Main features of the social system of the back streets

1 The people

The description so far has concentrated on features which the families have in common. They all consist of mother, father, and children, or mother and children living and eating together. We do not find the pattern common in many parts of the Middle East, where several married couples, usually agnatically related, compose a joint household. It is true that two of the seventeen families live with the husband's parents, but in both cases they have their own clearly separated rooms within the flat, and cook for themselves. Women and children have all their meals in the home, and the men most of theirs. All members of the families are primarily dependent on the head of the family and his income for their maintenance. In the few cases where teenage children have an income, this income, as mentioned above, is used for their personal expenses. Moreover, the family members form a unit – a corporation[1] – whenever one member is involved in quarrels with the outside world and when daughters are given away in marriage (Chapter 6). The basis of this solidarity is the idea that the family shares in a joint honour, in the sense that each member reaps honour and shame from the acts which other members of the family commit.

Internally, the interaction of the family members is organized in complementary roles as husband – wife, father-child, sister-brother, etc. Two roles are complementary when the duties of one party constitute the rights of the other and vice versa. But the activities of each individual are not only determined by his or her membership

---

[1] Corporation: a collectivity with joint responsibility and joint rights controlled by the members. This concept is useful in an anthropological analysis, because it helps us distinguish the groups within a community which can act as if they were a legal 'person'.

in the family as a corporation. For some important purposes, such as friendships, they behave as independent people who are free to enter into the relationships which they choose. Moreover, all adults retain their membership in their natal family as a continuing corporation. In both the family of birth and the family of marriage, each person has certain rights and assets, such as the right to claim support against the outside world. However, this also means that demands can be made on them from both directions. Since such demands do not concern exclusive rights, but rather help in the form of moral support, financial loans, practical help, etc., the possibility is not excluded that several people will make similar demands on the same person. In principle they are not incompatible. But poor people in Cairo face a special problem. Because resources are so scarce, both as regards material goods and loyalty and trust, as people see it, and because almost all relationships involve the demand that such obligations should be met, people are constantly exposed to conflicting pressures. They often feel that any manifestation of obligation shown in one direction reduces their potential for providing it in another direction. Thus, giving in one relationship becomes almost a denial of one's obligations in another. A strategic solution to this dilemma would be an attempt to control information, so that rival claimants in other relationships do not know what is being given. But this could only aggravate the situation further. All parties, after all, know that the *relation* to the others exists, and without any information they will *imagine* what is being given, letting their fears form their fantasies. They will exaggerate the threat to the possibility of getting something themselves, which these other people represent. The material illustrates the way in which people living in this area tend to interpret every fragment of information about people close to them in terms of this fear.

It seems to follow from these structural conditions, and it appears from the material I have collected, that people in such a social system have great difficulty in controlling the frame of interpretation imposed on their actions by others. Someone may try to fulfil a legitimate obligation, only to find that his action is interpreted quite differently by a third person, or even by the object of the exercise. If the participants in such a social system mistrust each other, they will constantly interpret each other's actions in the least advantageous light, and see them egocentrically as repudiation or treason against themselves. The structural preconditions of extreme discord and dissent seem to be present in such an organizational pattern.

Main features of the social system of the back streets   43

The dilemmas which arise and the patterns of action and conflict which are created, however, are also to a great extent determined by the identity of persons as man or woman, and the different rights and standards which these identities imply.

2. The shaping of gender roles – cultural ideals and realities

In Egyptian culture, man and woman are defined as fundamentally different kinds of persons. A man should be independent and not show respect to any men except those older than himself; he should be authoritative and domineering. He should always be on guard against insinuations from others that he lacks these qualities, and be prepared to defend his honour. He should prefer the company of men and not spend time with women. On the other hand, this view of masculinity does not imply any strict demands for responsibility and self-discipline; on the contrary it permits, perhaps even expects, the man to give priority to his own pleasure and enjoyment. Consequently, he can preserve an intimate, almost infantile relationship with his mother throughout his life, and he can be preoccupied with finding joy and masculine recognition from other women as sex parters.

Men monopolize women: as wives, unmarried sisters, or daughters. Friendship across the sex divide between unrelated people of opposite sex is prohibited. A husband has the monopoly of his wife's sexual attentions and of the work she and her daughters do. But these privileges also entail financial and social obligations towards women and children. The man should provide for them materially and look after and protect them against the rest of the world. As long as a husband fulfils these obligations towards his family, he has the right to take up to four wives. Women, on the other hand, cannot demand a divorce.

The woman's qualities complement those of the man: she should be humble, obedient, loyal, and deferential. Her position in the world is a reflection of her guardian's position. It is extremely shameful if financial need should drive a woman to work outside the home – that would be to publicize her husband's failure as a provider. On the other hand, it is becoming increasingly acceptable for a woman to take a job which gives prestige because it demands education. However, it is not through her work that a woman can realize herself. The essential confirmation of a woman's value is expressed through the material goods she obtains. She is fulfilled by being cared for, protected, cherished – that is according to this system of interpretation, by being loved. With the lack of intimacy between the sexes and the prohibition against any public display of tenderness, the only objective public scales for measuring love are material things. To give something of material value *means* to care, i.e. to love.

It follows from these codifications of gender roles that man and woman are linked in a fundamental, mutual dependence. As dependent as the woman is on the economic and legitimizing (status-bringing) benefits from the man, equally dependent is he on the woman's sexuality, work, and respect. In one sense he is the more dependent, as revealed by the fact that adult single men never live alone, dependent as they are on the work a woman does in the home. Divorced women and widows, however, can live in independent households. Three women out of the seventeen families in the study do this.

These codifications of gender roles determine the reciprocal rights of men and women, and entail standards for their self-presentation[1] and role enactment.

The critical factor for a poor population must be to what extent these standards imply or even require control of material resources for their fulfilment. There is a marked contrast between men on the one hand and women and children on the other in this respect. The man's role enactment *requires* material assets. He has obligations as the sole provider for his wife and children, and he can only assert his independence and compete for status among other men if he has material assets at his disposal. Women and children, on the other hand, do not in principle need such assets to fulfil their roles. Their services towards the husband are of an intangible kind (respect, loyalty, deference). But for their rank they are dependent within the community on the economic position created for them by the man.

The description in the two previous chapters has documented the man's failure in his role as main provider for the family he has founded. His dilemma, however, is even more profound because throughout his life he has financial obligations, legally sanctioned, to his family of birth: a needy mother or sister, a father unable to work, the children of a dead father or brother. Moreover, he has a moral obligation to be absolutely loyal. Social life in this poor neighbourhood, as the following chapters will show, has a way of

---

[1] I.e. the person's attempt to emphasize valued qualities about himself. This concept will appear throughout the book. It emphasizes another side of the theatrical model of social life (p. 24), that is, how we also in daily life make use of techniques like those of an actor when we want to give the impression that we are a certain type of person or that we have certain characteristics.

Main features of the social system of the back streets

frequently calling upon these obligations. This is not only due to death and divorce, but also to the fact that everyone at all times has too little and sees themselves as needy compared to others. The result is a situation of intense competition between the persons to whom the man has obligations – mainly between the women in his families of birth and marriage respectively. Not only does each little attention of his provoke jealousy in everyone else, but even the object of the attention will suspect the man of fulfilling less than he could, since she knows that he is being coerced from the other side. Therefore information control – i.e. secrecy – does not become an adequate solution for the man. The woman will refer to her rivals and evaluate the man's actions in the light of his relations to them.

However, it is rarely the man himself who is blamed for his failures. The relationship to him is extremely highly valued, indeed so highly that women will not admit a sign that love is lacking on his side. Instead, they put the blame on others, so as to protect the cherished relationship. Among the poor the man is seen primarily as manipulated (*taslīt*) by other women and controlled by them, and women are seen as the cause of, and given the blame for, everything the men do wrong. *Only on one single occasion* have I heard a woman, Umm Ali, maintain the theory that if a man makes a mistake *he himself* is to blame, because he has his own brain!

There are several reasons why a woman does not experience the same dilemma of cross-cutting obligations to her two families. Her obligations are non-material ones, such as work, favours, respect, and moral support, and these are not scarce in the way material resources are. Fulfilling her obligations to one person does not automatically exclude her from fulfilling similar obligations to other people. Moreover, her priorities are clearly stated: her husband's demands must come first. This is sanctioned both legally and morally. Consequently, the main structural feature of her position is the rivalry with her husband's family, not conflicting loyalties to two corporations.

The statuses that make up a relationship are necessarily reciprocal in the sense that one person's right is the other's obligation, and balance in the relationship depends on contributions from both sides. This has far-reaching consequences for the families among the poor. The wife feels her husband fails in his most fundamental obligation to her and the children: to provide them with the most necessary of food and clothing. For this the man must take the blame, for among his neighbours she is convinced she can see many examples of men in similar situations who are more successful, so that in this case she cannot blame her female rivals for his lack of success. Since she does not receive her due, she does not feel obliged to fulfill her duties to him: submissiveness and loyalty. But the woman's situation is further complicated by the fact that she needs material provision from her husband for many different purposes: not only is it seen as the direct and unequivocal expression of his love for her, and therefore as a measure for herself of her value as a human being, but it also serves to document this to other people. On their side the men resent this conception among the women. They say the deplorable result is that the women borrow and throw money to the winds just to be able to brag to the neighbour's wife: 'Look what my husband has given me!' – for example, going to the fish market when the fish is most expensive just to show off.

Material resources also constitute the woman's platform in her competition for recognition within the local environment. For this reason, women show the exaggerated interest which we have already seen in what the husbands of other women bring home, both in the form of goods and of money which they see converted into goods. Meanwhile they are constantly preoccupied with condemning the same kind of interest directed by others at themselves. The exceptions are the few occasions when they do have something to show; then it is extremely important to publicize it.

Since the woman's potential for achieving social recognition is to such a great extent undermined by her husband's material failure, her one chance of improving her position is to turn to means which she herself can control. These must remain secondary to that which legally and culturally defines her status, i.e. her husband's position, but by making use of them she can escape an unsatisfactory situation in which she depends completely on her husband for her identity.

The alternative to the material scale of value offered by this culture is a moral scale, religiously sanctioned, which emphasizes submission to God's will, and individual moral behaviour as the highest good. By appealing to this the woman can seek recognition from others for her personal moral qualities. This takes place in small circles created by friendship and alliances, and represents the most important sector of the women's social activity. Such activity mainly takes the form of intense gossiping where few chances are overlooked to slander others and praise oneself on a moral scale (see Chapter 8).

In other words, to realize herself, the woman makes the most of

Main features of the social system of the back streets 47

her independence as an individual and her moral qualities, rather than expressing her loyalty and solidarity with her husband. The pattern which emerges is one in which domineering women openly criticize their husbands, even to his face, in front of his friends, relatives, and children. Thus the woman violates her first obligation as a wife and mother: to teach the children respect for their father. She also refuses to obey his commands regarding how the daily problems of the household should be solved, such as borrowing money only when he permits it, i.e. when there is no risk of his losing face. People themselves summarize this pattern in these expressions: 'With us the man obeys his wife' (*irrāgil biyīsmaç kalām mirātu*). 'With us the man totters after his wife' (*hina irrāgil māshi wara mirātu*). 'Here it is women who rule' (*issittāt biyuḥkumu*).

3. Generalizations about fellow human beings

We have seen that even the most intimate relations within the family unit become problematical because none of the parties involved fulfil their obligations. This is one aspect of a more general experience and expectation amongst the poor: that people in most social relations, with the one categorical exception of the mother-child relationship, are opportunist, false, and dangerous. This view exists as an explicit premise for all social interaction and is constantly confirmed to them through their experiences in all areas of life. Social interaction in the poor quarter becomes easier to understand if we consider these cultural premises as they are expressed by the poor themselves. I shall describe them partly by using the Arabic key-phrases, and partly by paraphrasing direct statements. In subsequent chapters I shall then attempt to describe the processes whereby these premises are generated and confirmed.

Fellow human beings fall into two main categories: Christians and Moslems. They are seen as entirely different kinds of people. Christians co-operate and help each other, they have compassion (*Ilmesīḥiyyīn biyiçmily gamçiyya wa biysāçdu bāçd. 'anduhum mawaḍḍa*). The Moslems, on the other hand, have no love for their fellow-man, no one cares about anyone else nowadays, (*maḥaddish biyisa'al çala ḥadd innaharda*) – there is no co-operation (*mafīsh taçawun*). 'If a man sees his brother starving in the street, he won't give him as much as a piece of bread.' 'If you ask your brother to lend you some money, he'll say he hasn't got any.' Everyone evades obligations and 'only acts in their own interest' (*biyshūfu maslaḥathum bass*). If you should have anything of value to them, they will come running to assure you how much they love you. The minute they see that there is no more to be had, they all lose interest and leave you. 'They only love me because of the money' (*biyḥibbūni çashan ilfulūs bass*) expresses the bitter experience of many people.

People are not only opportunists, 'they are also intensely envious'. People will curse anyone they see who is better than themselves (*ilçenén biyikraḥu illi aḥsan minnu*). They will try to put obstacles in his way and rob him of what he values. Yes, the Moslems never wish each other anything good at all (*il Muslimīn mish biyḥibbu ilxér li baçd abadan*). 'If, for example, two women are friends, people will most certainly try to alienate them'. They will try to cause harm in two different ways: by *xobs* or *kalám innás*. *Xobs* is a deliberate distortion of the truth, lies (*kixb*), slander. It can be done for example by quoting a person but exaggerating 100 times (*biyaxdu ikkalám wa biyzīdū mīt marrāt*). *Kalám innás* is a dangerous, powerful social process where 'people torment the life out of each other'. In direct translation the words mean 'people's talk' but this talk has a very definite character, which is clearly institutionalized: (i) an orientation implying a constant gathering of information about others, (ii) every tiny fragment of information being interpreted in the worst sense possible, (iii) the information thus interpreted becoming a social fact in communication with others, (iv) this criticism poisoning and tarnishing the whole environment. Due to *kalám innás* people have no freedom/autonomy (*mafīsh ḥurriya*).

People are unreliable and dangerous for one more reason: 'they have two faces (*wishshén*), one in front of you, one behind your back'. Therefore, 'you should never trust them'. 'They can even share bread and salt with you and yet deceive you at the next moment'. They are deceitful (*xayranīn*). They are also mean (*buxala*) and greedy (*gaçanīn*) and fail in their most fundamental human obligation: to show hospitality. 'They hide their food under the bed or cupboard when you come, just to avoid sharing it with you'. 'And when they invite you, they do so because they must, not because they want to.' 'At the next moment you risk being put to shame by them because of the food' (*yiçayru fil akl*). 'They will go round condemning you for being so gluttonous, as if you didn't have money for food yourself!'

Briefly, people (Moslems) have no conscience any more (*mafīsh damīç,/zimma*), neither rich nor poor. But it is easier to understand with the poor, since 'hunger drives them to sell their conscience for money'. 'All they can think of is food and money

Main features of the social system of the back streets   49

[and sleep, according to male informants]. They say: *'Allahu Akbar* – God is great – and cheat each other unscrupulously, rich as well as poor.' 'The grocer will mix potato into his butter', 'the butcher water into his meat', 'the doctors water into the medicine bottles', 'at the hospital they'll give you one injection instead of the ten prescribed and sell the rest'. 'Ministers and other high officials get rich at your expense; they took, for example, the boxes of butter and milk sent by America as a *gift* to the poor, and sold them'. 'Each year they will have a "winter collection for the poor" (*maōqnit ishshīta* – food and clothes) but the poor never see any of it.' 'There is no system or order at all in this country' (*mafīsh nizám xalis*). The pattern is: 'Egyptians eat each other like fish' (*Ilmaṣriyyīn biyaklu fi baçyd zavy issamak*).

These experiences naturally lead to the formulation of certain acknowledged rules for living: 'Mix with others as little as possible.' 'Be always careful with what you say and do.' 'Don't trust anyone,' that is, 'don't let yourself be taken in by impressions.'

The best thing a woman can do is to keep the door to her flat closed and visit no one.' Each visit gives the hostess the opportunity to go round afterwards, saying: 'In the name of the Prophet, can you imagine what she came to me and said . . . !' (implying came *to* say). And you cannot defend yourself, for after all you *were* there! 'You also risk, and can't defend yourself against it, that others blame *you* if she gets into conflict with them;' they will say 'you manipulated her' (*enti illi sallaṭīha*) – 'If you visit anyone, never accept any food. If you become enemies, which can happen at any time, she will shame you in front of all the world saying you ate the food for the children because you were so poor you couldn't afford food for yourself!'

The best protection for a man is to practice careful information control – by keeping other people at arm's length – and by 'stopping friends/acquaintances coming to your home'. Each visit offers the guest the possibility of going out and revealing the family's secrets (*yīgib ṣirr ilbēt*), saying that 'the furniture was ugly, the wife was ugly', etc.

These accusations, generalizations, and rules probably have their equivalents in other cultures. But what is here so characteristic is that they quite consistently confirm and reinforce each other, that they seem to dominate as a general view of man, and that they are ubiquitously applied as the basis of all human intercourse.

4. The men's arenas

Men can move around freely. They can come and go as they like without being compromised. Daily activities take them from home to work, back home or to a café for lunch, to the extra job and/or to the café, and then home again to bed. The pattern is slightly different for those who have a television set. They will spend more of their spare time at home. But men generally are ill at ease in the home: it is crowded, there is no fresh air, the children are noisy. Some say themselves that they soon get irritated and beat the children.

Men in general have little spare time. What they have, however, is usually spent with friends in cafés. Friendship is established at the place of work, not in the neighbourhood. The expressions of friendship are material gifts such as cigarettes and tea – without any formal accounting – and also small loans, and moral and physical support against the rest of the world. Men do not provide jobs for each other, they can only lend a hand by telling each other about jobs that are advertised. Sometimes they may give each other some special service in connection with their jobs, like the mechanic who always repairs his driver's-friend's car first. The loyalty in these relationships, however, seems to be rather shallow. According to the men themselves, their friendships have the same unstable character as those of the women (see parts 3 and 5 of this chapter, and Chapter 6).

Men from the same back street or quarter do not belong to any common organization. There is no occasion at all when they get together by virtue of their membership in one common neighbourhood.

Each man likes to have a café where he is a regular customer. There is a wide choice: for there are plenty of cafés in all quarters. Most of the cafés are in the main streets, but some are at the corners of back streets. Each café has a name which serves as a contact address for regular customers' friends and acquaintances. There is no clear pattern for the choice of a favourite café, and men from the same neighbourhood do not stick together. But many men choose one fairly near home so that children can run there with messages. Friends visit each other in each others' cafés. I do not know how frequent or how long these visits may be. In front of women the men try to pretend they do not go, often using the phrase: 'Cafés cost money'. What they refer to is the man's obligation to buy drinks for friends (and acquaintances?) who pass his table. Others claim they go to the café only to watch television – that will cost them the price of a cup of tea, 1½p. Others deny that they go at all by emphasizing the morally unacceptable activity which takes place there: gambling. But on the whole, all men say they *like* to sit in a café: there is fresh air, and it is relaxing and

Main features of the social system of the back streets 51

entertaining to watch life in the street. The details about their extra jobs imply, however, that their time in cafés is limited; observations from a distance show that the clientèle in cafés consists mostly of young lads and older men.

Men hardly ever bring home unrelated friends. Only in case of illness should a man go to his friend's house, to wish him a speedy recovery. He will then be offered a glass of tea, stay for a moment and then leave. Men give several reasons why they do not want their friends to visit them at home:

(1) A visit calls for attention – which means extra expense.
(2) They are ashamed of the flat, and afraid that the friend might reveal these dark secrets to a wider circle. (*Yigīb sirr ilbēt* = reveal the secrets of the family/house.)
(3) Lack of space. Friends need a room where they can sit in peace. The flat is full of children and noise.
(4) Protection of the wife – fear that the friend might catch a glimpse of the wife and desire her.
(5) Fear that the wife might catch a glimpse of the friend and get the impression that the friend's financial position is better than his own. This would lead to further accusations and nagging from her.
(6) The flat is a place for women to meet; men meet in the cafés.

Though the men are physically absent from the back streets for most of the time, they play an important role in local social organization, both by linking people together, thus defining groups, and by the actions they perform when they are home: they (i) provide material resources and status, (ii) are the formal spokesmen and defenders of the families, (iii) mediate in marital conflicts involving close female relatives, (iv) are themselves part of marital conflicts involving other men as mediators.

The man's presence in the home will affect the situation in that he exerts authority over the children in a much tougher and more definite way than does the mother. Moreover, he is usually tired and irritable when he comes home and this affects the atmosphere. The wife stays in the flat to serve his needs, and her unrelated women friends, who usually walk in and out freely, become more reserved and limit their visits. Her blood relations, however – mother and sisters – will rarely let themselves be abashed by the husband's presence. Any confrontations between households which have taken place during his absence are related by the wife and are given an authoritative form as men confront each other in defence of each household. The course of events usually follows this pattern: children fight, the mothers respectively confront each other in defence of their children, the mothers then complain to their husbands, and the men attack each other, often even with knives. After each such event the men insist that their wives and children should stay in the flats.

The man's close relations come rarely or never to his home. If they need him, they will send a child with a message that he should go to them. When he decides to go and see them, he will go alone or with his small children. It does happen that a woman is temporarily on speaking terms with – or even a sort of friend of – her sister-in-law and goes with her husband to visit, especially if the sister-in-law has a television set and she herself has not. But in most cases the women avoid their in-laws. Sometimes, however, the residence arrangements are such that explosive conflicts break out and call for a solution from the man: eight of the seventeen families have shared or are sharing a flat with the husband's mother or sister. In six of these cases life soon became so unbearable that the husband took the formal initiative and moved out. In the two cases where a family is still sharing a flat with the man's family, the solution to the problem seems to be for the mother-in-law and the wife to be more or less permanently not on speaking terms.

In marital conflicts it is the men who, by virtue of their authority, assume the role of mediators. Although they represent family units and interested parties, they try to keep to rules of relevance and objectivity which contrast sharply with the women's style, which has few rules of relevance. In that way they can reach a solution which is acceptable to all and settle the conflict – until the next crossroads. This, however, does not stop them giving quite a different, partial presentation of the conflict and their own role on a later occasion, in front of another audience, when their style is very much like that of the women, as I see it.

The following course of events can serve as a concrete example of the role of men as mediators. Their attitude to women in general shows up clearly, especially in regard to their own mothers. Umm Hussein is twenty-two years old, and married to Abdullah, twenty-seven. They share a flat with Abdullah's parents and brother. Abdullah pays the rent for all. Umm Hussein has no relatives in the neighbourhood, her mother is dead, and her father lives in Alexandria. Her nearest contact and best friend is Umm Mohammed. Umm Mohammed's husband, Ahmed, is Abdullah's best friend. But Umm Hussein's in-laws are arch enemies of Umm Mohammed and her family (mother and sisters). Therefore the two friends always used to meet in Umm Mohammed's house. But one day Umm Mohammed came into Umm Hussein's room and stayed for about ten minutes to share with her some clothes I had given them. To avoid being seen by Umm Hussein's arch enemy, a cousin, from her roof across the lane, they hung a rug in front of the window, and locked the door of the flat safely. The cousin saw the rug and suspected mischief. At first she sent up her children to listen by the door. Then she herself came tearing down, broke open the lock on the door, and found both the clothes and Umm Mohammed. Knowing full well that Umm Hussein's in-laws would be furious if they knew that the arch enemy had set foot in their son's flat, she made sure they found out. And the row that followed was everything she could have wished for. The mother-in-law was furious with her son, Abdullah, who beat his wife and told her to go away in the middle of the night: 'You bitch, you whore, I'm divorcing you! Go away! I don't want you! Go and work as a washer-woman or a maid! Provide for yourself! That's all you deserve!'

Umm Hussein cried desperately but stayed in the flat. She dared not leave in case Abdullah took her furniture and sold it (see p. 84). The next morning she sent the children with money to Umm Mohammed so that she could send a telegram to Umm Hussein's father. The telegram should say especially that Abdullah had refused to let her go and see her father (which was actually true). By appealing to her father's pride in this way, she hoped to mobilize him in spite of her stepmother's advice to him to do the opposite. She did not *expect* her father to come, for 'the husband does what the wife says'.

But this time the father did come. During the mediation which followed, Umm Hussein's father, Umm Hussein and Abdullah, Abdullah's younger brother, and myself were all present. The main issue was whether or not Umm Hussein had acted against her husband's orders by admitting her friend to the flat. Everybody agreed that since Abdullah pays the rent for the flat (where his parents and younger brothers also live) *he* decides who can set foot in it.

Abdullah's brother said that if Abdullah approved of Umm Mohammed being in his flat, he and Abdullah could no longer be brothers, because Umm Mohammed had called their mother 'thirty times a whore'. Abdullah said he did not approve. Umm Hussein corrected him and defended herself by saying that he had never *refused* Umm Mohammed access to the flat, and she had said to him that if he wanted to do this, he would have to tell Umm Mohammed himself. Abdullah dodged the challenge and instead attacked for her running about all the time, even after he bought her a television set to keep her indoors. Moreover, he had asked her emphatically not to mix with neighbours (not mentioning any names) because every man knows the result of women's talk (*kalám issittát*). 'Yes,' Umm Hussein's father put in, 'I've told you you *must* avoid the neighbours to live in peace. And he is your husband. If he forbids you, you must obey.'

Umm Hussein pointed out that Abdullah had never forbidden her to see Umm Mohammed. But in spite of that, she sees her friend much less now than before, although she finishes her housework at ten o'clock in the morning and has nothing to do for the rest of the day. 'But it doesn't matter what I do or don't. They [i.e. the mother-in-law and sister-in-law] will say: "She keeps running across there all the time!" whatever I do.'

Abdullah's brother explained that it is quite acceptable for Umm Hussein to see her other neighbours. It is only Umm Mohammed's family that she must avoid, because they are such dreadful people. Umm Hussein replied that Abdullah and Ahmed (Umm Mohammed's husband) are friends. In that case why can't she . . ?

The brother-in-law said: 'Because Ahmed comes from a completely different family. He is the son of educated people (*ibn insān*) – the others are beasts. *That's* why I didn't tell mother when Ahmed came to see Abdullah to watch television, when his own was broken! And that time he quarrelled with us [an enormous row between Ahmed and Abdullah's brother about a year ago when they hurt each other seriously and were taken to the police station], it was because he was manipulated by the women. It's the *women* we have to separate. Didn't Umm Hussein herself say that time that she was afraid of being alone at home, because Umm Mohammed's family might break the door open and attack her physically?'

Umm Hussein denied this. (However I was there when this incident took place and I can confirm that the brother-in-law was telling the truth.)

Umm Hussein's father then talked, reproaching Abdullah for not yet having found a flat for himself and Umm Hussein. They had known for a long time that it was necessary, both because of the problems with in-laws in the same flat, and in order to get Umm Hussein away from Umm Mohammed. And then Umm Hussein will have to stay in the flat all the time! It's all right for men to see each other but women . . . !

The mediation ended with everyone agreeing that Abdullah should look round for another flat when he next got his wages.

Before leaving, Umm Hussein's father asked Abdullah never again to beat his daughter. 'Do promise, or else she'll come and live with me. I want her to have a happy life.' He also gave his daughter some money so that she could come to Alexandria on her own if there was another conflict.

5. The women's arenas and life situations

A woman's life unfolds mainly in her own home, in the back streets adjacent to it, and in the homes of half a dozen other women. Her freedom of movement is limited by her husband to this neighbourhood. Even inside it the husband has a right to control her freedom, but rarely takes advantage of this right, as long as (i) her relationships do not involve the family in conflict, and (ii) she or a grown-up daughter are always there when he comes home. This last demand is so categorical that once it lead to threats of divorce and dismissal of the wife when the husband returned to an empty house, although the reason for her absence was that the wife was assisting her friend on the floor above in childbirth. On the other hand their flat seems to be regarded as *her* territory: she is the housewife (*sitt ilbêt*) and only she can offer food or drink to guests. The husband's family regard it as her house and so avoid visiting.

Inside this restricted living space the woman is constantly observed in whatever she does, and we have seen how greedy the neighbours are for such information. A typical example is this: Umm Hussein was standing outside the door of her house, telling a friend that so far she had had nothing new for the feast after Ramadan. The information came back to her in the form of criticism and abuse from the mother-in-law. It turned out that Umm Hussein's cousin and enemy had overheard the conversation from the roof of her house across the lane and immediately passed it on to the place where it would harm Umm Hussein the most.

The woman has no secure 'back stage' for herself or her family. There are even cases where people have broken into a flat while the housewife was out, as part of faction intrigues. (See p. 132). Many of the woman's daily activities can be best understood in the context of her competition for recognition in the back street environment. Her main rivals are her relatives, closest neighbours, and in-laws. What they are all seeking is confirmation from others that they are more highly valued than their rivals. A woman achieves such confirmation by responses which can best be summarized as recognition: others turning to her for company, praising her in front of third parties, and being willing to admire the material gifts she chooses to show them. But the folk generalizations summarized in part 3 of this chapter complicate such intercourse, both because many people systematically mistrust the woman's intentions and spread evil-minded interpretations of her actions, and because she herself interprets their reactions to her with the same distrust. I shall develop this theme in Chapter 8. Here I will mainly give an outline of the arenas where such activities take place.

The main sources of recognition are material gifts. When a woman walks down the street with a pair of new shoes, when she carries parcels whose contents can be identified (which is nearly always possible due to standardized wrappings) she can reach a large, diffuse audience with a message of her success. But such occasions are quite rare, and most of the time the woman must be content to obtain recognition merely by what people say when they praise her with reference to a moral rather than material standard. For most of these confirmations she has to turn to the small circles which she herself can create or to which she can gain access: friendships, acquaintances, and alliances.

These small groups can form because the woman is not tied to continuous work. Her daily routine is to bring up the children, do the shopping, cook, clean, and wash clothes. The cooking usually takes about three hours, occasionally four to five. This means women have plenty of spare time. And since the husband is absent most of the time, she is not tied to the flat. Small children can be brought along anywhere, regardless of time.

To be alone, moreover, is seen in this culture as undesirable and unbearable. If left alone, therefore, a woman will seek the company of others, and she likes to form friendships. The choice of friends by the seventeen women in the study shows a characteristic and clear pattern: nine of them have their closest woman-friend(s) in the same house as their own or the house across the road. This gives them company while not causing them to neglect any of their obligations as housewives; they can keep an eye out for possible visitors and receive them. It is shameful to 'run around'. Of the remaining eight women, five spend most of their time with a relative living nearby; mother, daughter, or sister. Only one has a best friend who lives a few streets away, but this friendship started when they were next-door neighbours. One has very little social life because she works hard outside the home and spends her free time with her child, and another has chosen to dissociate herself from the neighbourhood by isolating herself (see p. 146).

This relation to women-friends provides a woman with the best and most regularly used forum for obtaining social recognition.

Main features of the social system of the back streets

The interaction of two such friends shows a characteristic pattern. Children, from new-born babies to children of ten or twelve, often come with their mother to visit. Infants are always brought along. The children play in the flat with the hostess's children or outside the house. The women go shopping together, and often cook together (cleaning rice, beans, etc.). But most of the time they just sit talking together, interrupted by children screaming and fussing. Four themes dominate these conversations: (i) *Money* – counted coin by coin, what they have, have spent, do not have but should have, etc. The theme can hardly be discussed without the husband being criticized. (ii) *Food* – they tell each other in minute detail what they have just eaten, will eat, should eat, dream about eating, etc. (iii) *The husband* – he is criticized or condemned in a comparison which explicitly or implicitly emphasises the woman's superior moral and intellectual qualities, such as sense of responsibility, ability to economize, and intelligence. (iv) *Gossip* – the actions of other women are interpreted and criticized. Conversations about this theme and, to a certain extent, the previous one, give the best opportunities for the woman to present herself as a morally superior and completely blameless person. Every characterization of others is put in such a way that it, explicitly or implicitly, can be turned into an emphasis of her own assets. These are two characteristic examples:

(1) Umm Gamal was telling two friends about her sister-in-law, Zenab: 'Her little girl was ill, so she took her to see a doctor and came back to her husband, saying: "The doctor says she needs nutritious food" [i.e. meat, milk, eggs, cheese, etc. – expensive and status-bringing food]. By God, as if *she* needs nutritious food! All Zenab ever does is demand from her husband the same things as the neighbour gets from hers – when it is her obvious *duty* in life to make do with whatever her husband gives her!'

(2) Umm Foad said to me (in connection with Ramadan) about a mutual acquaintance who has recently got herself a job: 'Can you *imagine*, Umm Ali has made *masses* of cakes! 15-16 kgs.!'

I said: 'That's not true. I haven't seen any.'

'By the Prophet, it *is* true, but Umm Ali is mean and won't tell anyone.'

I said: 'I'm *sure* she hasn't made any this year.'

'Oh well, maybe – because she *works* and doesn't have the time this year. But she usually makes lots *every year!*'

Umm Foad here tried to establish (i) that Umm Ali is prodigal and immoral, whilst she herself is economical and virtuous, and unintentionally I gave her the opportunity to establish (ii) that

Umm Ali is a greedy liar, whilst she herself is honest and hospitable, and also (iii) – for the hundredth time, she could condemn Umm Ali's lack of morals and lowliness in going out to work. In other words, my interpretation of this gossip is as follows: when a woman purveys gossip she is actually more concerned with her own self-presentation[1] than with the person she is slandering. The gossip serves as a way for her to emphasize her own valued characteristics, and of obtaining confirmation from her audience of her cherished self-image. But indirectly, the gossip also serves as a form of social control since all women at all times fear what others might say about them. Measured in time, it dominates the conversations.

Sometimes the conversation between two friends will be interrupted by a third friend, a relative or acquaintance of the hostess, who drops by on some errand or other: it may be to borrow something, complain about someone they all know, or seek support for her own self-image, tell some news, etc. If the guest is unrelated and /or a rare guest, the hostess will insist on serving her tea or juice, and tries to force her friend also to accept. If the guest stays on, another attentive audience is established, where each woman present can display her own moral excellence through criticism of other people, and be sure of having her self-image confirmed. It is doubtful, however, whether the newcomer would support the original two friends in front of another audience, or they her.

Sudden changes in the background noise from the street outside always attract the women's attention. Boisterous, explosive rows between adults occur almost every day. The immediate reason for such conflicts is usually fights between the children when the mothers rush in defence of their own, reproach each other, and hurl insults in proportion to the value they set on the relations between them. If their own or their friends' children are involved, this gives an opportunity to confirm friendship and recognition by a show of loyalty.

What are the features which distinguish friendship from other types of relations? How do two women-friends express their relationship?

The women themselves emphasise intimacy (*ixṭilāṭ*) devotion (*mawadda*), and trust (*thiqqa*) as the conditions for real friendship. A friend should love you and seek your company only for your own sake, not for opportunist reasons. And you must be able to trust her always to do what is best for you, even when you are not around yourself. Proof of the existence of this quality in a

---

[1] See footnote on p.44.

Main features of the social system of the back streets 59

relationship is the unconditional support shown by the friend against the rest of the world. She should also unconditionally accept and reinforce her friend's self-image. It is in the nature of this demand that it comprises the whole person, not only a part-status, and thus mutual friendship between three women is impossible: in trifling disagreements between two of them, both would demand total support from the third one. This woman could not then avoid behaving in a way that would be seen as partial by one of the two conflicting parties. It is, however, possible to have several friends, provided there is no close personal relationship between them.

Ideally, a friend is always prepared to incur expenses to help out in difficulties. On ritual occasions and in cases of illness she should confirm the friendship by observing conventions regarding gifts and visits with standardized good wishes or condolences, a custom which no other person except the mother (and perhaps brother) regularly fulfils.

In contrast to the folk generalizations about people being always deceitful and opportunistic, the relationship between friends is afforded a strong positive value. This brings about a strongly inflated friendship ideal. Except for the relationship mother-child, it is from the personal point of view the most satisfying social relation. This is expressed by women-friends saying about each other: 'I love her more than my own sister' or 'As a friend, she is like a sister to me.' The standard expression used to emphasize the noble character of a friend is: 'She's very good – she loves me.' (*Kwayyisa qawi, bithibbini*). It is characteristic that moral values are judged from an egocentric point of view, as kindness towards one's self, rather than to people in general.

Ideally, friendship is based on complete trust. But each person has numerous experiences of the risk implied by a trust relation. For this reason most friendships are in fact marked by mistrust and prevarications. The plainest expression of this is an insistence on the part of many (most?) women not to accept food in a friend's house. This *may* be an expression of mutual adjustment to a situation of unpredictable scarcity. But it is also an irrefutable fact that the acceptance of hospitality gives the other woman a trump card in a possible future conflict (see pp. 49 and 135).

Because friendship is so highly valued, the general opinion is that people from jealousy try to destroy other people's friendships. Their common tactic is to go to one of the people involved and tell lies about the friend. Certainly, friendships do break up, both for this reason and others. And I interpret the fact that ex-friends after such a break almost immediately throw themselves into attempts to find one or several scapegoats, and refuse to accept the break as the expression of lack of love from the other woman's side, unless there are obvious indications of this, as yet another proof of the high value attached to the friendship. The standard phrase is: 'She loves me, but because of such and such's manipulation . . .' (*Bithibbini, bass min ittaslit* . . .) I attach the same interpretation to the fact that some ex-friends, after swearing each other eternal enmity – and sometimes even spreading around each other's most intimate confidences – can re-establish friendship.

6. Types of relationships and networks amongst women

Friendship is only one of the culturally recognized social relationships into which women enter. Their social world outside the home consists in addition of five main types of relationship:

(1) Female acquaintances (*maçrifa*) are categorically distinguished from friends due to the absence of *ixtilāt/mawadda* (intimacy/devotion). Acquaintances acknowledge their relationship by exchanging stereotype greetings or polite phrases when they meet, usually no more than 'good morning'. Some neighbours and some friends of friends and relatives of friends will fall into this category. Acquaintances can also be instrumental, for example, women will borrow kitchen utensils from each other.

(2) Relatives (*qarāyib*) have extensive, although diffusely defined, morally sanctioned rights to loyalty and assistance. There is an important distinction between relatives on the father's and the mother's side, with the latter as by far the most intimate. Thanks to their kinship relationship they have a right to visit the woman's home whenever they like. The general idea is that they come mainly in their own interest, for example to watch television. On the other hand, they are absent on most ritual occasions. This is summarized by the standard phrase: 'Relatives never love each other at all.' (*Ilqarāyib mish biyhibbu bāçd abadan*).

(3) In-laws (*nasáyib*) – the husband's mother and sisters and the wives of the woman's brothers are the most important characters in this category. The woman believes they are constantly preoccupied with trying to set her husband up against her/manipulating him (i.e. practise *taslít*) and vice versa: the husband's mother and sisters hardly ever visit the daughter/sister-in-law – and the pattern is for them to be absent on ritual occasions. It does, however, occur that a sister-in-law invades the house because of her brother's duty to provide for her in an emergency. However, due to the conflict-laden

Main features of the social system of the back streets

in-law relationship, such arrangements are always short-lived. (See p. 128).

(4) Enemies are characterized by not being on speaking terms (the word is *mitaxasmāha* – I'm not on speaking terms with her, derived from the noun *xisām* = quarrel). The condition is a result of a confrontation in which they either played the leading roles or identified themselves as opponents by letting themselves be mobilized on either side in the conflict. The standard phrase describing the reason for the conflict is 'the kids fought' (*Ilçayyāl ḍarábu báçd*). The behaviour of enemies towards each other is characterized by their constant search for an audience who will support the degradation of the opponent and praise their own blameless behaviour. The most accessible partners are people who have a bone to pick with the same enemy – and alliances around such mutual interests are always being formed (see pp. 138-9).

(5) Unknown women (*mish çarfáha* = I don't know her) are women living nearby whom the woman does not greet. Some of these may live in the same back street, possibly even in the same house.

The following chapters will show how the local social system is built on such categories and shaped by the choices which the participants make on the basis of what they themselves see as their options. But to provide a framework for the understanding of this, I would like to conclude by giving a summary of the women's total network of social relations through three examples. (The details were taken in August 1972.) The three women I choose are those whose social circles I am most familiar with:

(1) Umm Mohammed (twenty-six years old). Grew up in the neighbourhood and has many (over twenty) relatives there.
(2) Umm Ali (thirty-six years old). Moved into the neighbourhood fifteen years ago and has some (less than ten) relatives there.
(3) Umm Hussein (twenty-six years old). Moved into the neighbourhood eight years ago and has hardly any relatives.

Out of a potential of 4-5,000 people living within five minutes' walking distance from the homes of these three women, their whole social universe consists of forty-one, thirty-one, and twenty-seven people respectively. These figures do not include single young people, children, and some men whom the women only meet as the husbands of other women. In other words, the universe includes all the people with whom a woman has or could develop a personal relationship, and no others. These are mainly other women, but also include male relatives and in-laws (men who have married into her family, as well as the husband's family) with whom she can socialize freely. The category 'acquaintances' where Umm Ali is concerned only includes people I have either met in her house or heard her refer to approvingly. As regards Umm Mohammed and Umm Hussein, I believe I have elicited complete information about all the people they greet. In *Table 4(1)* below 'being on speaking terms' and 'not being on speaking terms' are shown by the signs + and − . But it is important to bear in mind that this division is not between an active personal relationship and an active enemy relationship. To 'be on speaking terms' here only means that two women recognize a positive relationship between them.

Table 4(1): *Patterns of enmity and friendship*

	+	−	total	the categories 'relatives' and 'in-laws' consist of the following people:
Umm Mohammed				
woman-friends	3		3	2 sisters, mother, mother's brother, his wife, mother's half-brother, mother's uncle, mother's 3 cousins, 2 cousins and their wives, husband's 3 sisters, husband's stepmother, own half-brother and his wife.
relatives	7	5	12	
in-laws	3	5	8	
acquaintances	18		18	
other enemies		5	5	
total	31	15	46	
Umm Ali				
women-friends	1		1	2 sisters, dead sister's son and daughter, brother, his wife, husband's sister and brother, husband's 2 nieces, stepmother, paternal cousin.
relatives	2	4	6	
in-laws	3	3	6	
acquaintances	12		12	
other enemies		6	6	
total	18	13	31	
Umm Hussein				
women-friends	3		3	Father, father's cousin + his daughter and cousin, cousin's mother, stepmother, mother-in-law, husband's mother + father + sister, 2 brothers + brother's wife.
relatives	3	2	5	
in-laws	2	5	7	
acquaintances	12		12	
other enemies				
total	20	7	27	

Main features of the social system of the back streets

Friendship and enmity vary, and in order to understand how stable these social networks are, we can study the duration of each relationship. One friendship in this sample is outstanding as very strong and stable – that of Umm Ali which has lasted for sixteen years with only two short breaks.[1] This realizes an ideal which none of the other sixteen women in the sample had experienced. The friendship relations of Umm Mohammed and Umm Hussein have had the following durations: one year, five years, one year; the third friendship for each of the women is the one which links Umm Mohammed and Umm Hussein. It was first formed six years ago, was broken due to conflict after three and a half years for about one and a half years, and was then re-established.

Enmities, exemplified by Umm Ali, show the following durations: sister – six years, dead sister's son – four years, dead sister's daughter – four years, mother's cousin – six months, brother's wife – one month, husband's sister's daughter – one year, close neighbour – two months, three years, neighbours in the same house – four years, two years, saving club chairman – eight months, brother's family – one month. The other two women show a similar pattern.

Regarding the frequency of contact, it is important to bear in mind that only a fraction of the people in the positive categories are in frequent touch with each other. Those who regularly come and 'sit down' in the woman's house (the criterion of a close relation) are no more than three to four people.

In other words, we see in this material a strikingly clear pattern of social organization. Without clear-cut corporations on a higher level than the family unit, the structure is best described as one large, connected network of social relations. In this urban mass of stably localized people, who superficially show such strong sociability and conviviality, the number of relationships which each person has is strikingly low. The people who actually form part of each person's active network are moreover constantly changing, primarily because frequent outbreaks of enmity lead to alternative links being formed as substitutes and/or alliances. When on two occasions I returned to the field after absences of about a year, the changes of personnel in networks and in enmity patterns were so extensive that on both occasions they strongly complicated my field work (see p. 138). The result of such processes is a characteristic form of disintegration of the neighbourhood as a social environment through a constant undermining of trust relationships.

---

[1] In the spring of 1975, however, it broke up again and four years later had not been re-established.

FIVE

Some of the children's social experiences whilst growing up

In this chapter I shall try to describe some fundamental features of children's life situations whilst growing up. The features which I emphasize are characteristic and typical but in no way representative of the total range of experience of a child. The selection has not been made in relation to any systematic theory of personality development. Neither is the material presented here compiled with a view to describing or analyzing the child's world. It is based on incidental observations which I made while I was living in the environment with the purpose of understanding the world of the adults.

The incentive to write this chapter did not appear until my last month of field work, when I felt that my main purpose had been achieved. I then had more time and interest for the children. Furthermore, some events took place which involved children in such a dramatic way that I could not help reacting with astonishment. The adults who noticed my reactions immediately remarked that such childhood experiences were shared by all in this culture, and then started to tell me about their own and other people's childhood memories. This made me ask: What effect do such childhood experiences have on personality development? How do they influence the adults' perception of themselves, the world, and other people?

In this chapter I shall try to suggest some answers. I have concentrated on certain patterns in the children's roles in relation to parents and brothers and sisters, and on some critical situations which dramatically enhance aspects of their identity and obligations. I find it reasonable to suggest that such experiences must affect children's views of themselves and others; and in these patterns I find exactly those features which so strongly distinguish the relations between adults in the poor quarter, that is, their

Some of the children's social experiences whilst growing up 65

general attitude of distrust and suspicion as well as other critical attitudes to their fellow beings that are embedded in their traditional folk wisdom. I find it reasonable to assume that these childhood experiences are important sources, besides the objective situation of poverty, of the patterns characterizing the back streets as a social system.

Children are socially defined by their father's position. This is explained by the fact that 'the blood comes from the father' (*iddamm min ilabb*). The first duty of a child is to its father: to obey him, respect, and honour him. Second, children should be polite and well mannered (*muaddab*) in social relations generally. Ammar (1954: 133) says: 'the main objective of child training is to cultivate a docile and yielding disposition in the child as the main characteristic of a "muaddab"'. This implies primarily that they show respect to all persons older than themselves, ideally even if the age difference is only a week (see Ammar p. 137: 'He who is one day older is in fact one year wiser'.) Knowledge, understanding, and wisdom are seen as proportionate to age. The family has a joint honour in which children partake as well as their parents. This entails the child's right to unconditional support from the parents against the rest of the world, no matter what the child has done. Finally, children have a right to economic support from the father until they are adults. Ideally, sons should then compensate their father for the food and lodgings they have received, but this ideal is fulfilled extremely seldom. (I have never heard of a single case.)

The mother has the principal responsibility for bringing up the children. The father and older brothers and sisters play very subsidiary roles. Moreover, the folk conception is that the mother *alone* forms the character of the child through her major role in the upbringing. Although the child's blood stems from its father, people do not count this as having any effect on the child's character.

In accordance with this, fathers regard the children as powerful weapons in their wives' hands. Depending on how the woman chooses to play her role as wife and mother, she can shape her children so that they come to show their father proper respect or no respect at all. As one father put it: 'By not obeying me and by being submissive to the children she gives them the impression that I am selfish and ruthless. One day they will hate me and sneer at my orders. And I shall no longer be master in my own house.' In this way the children become important pawns in a game between the parents, thus inevitably gaining an intimate experience of the lack of loyalty with the family unit.

Most of the children's social intercourse is with women and other children, primarily their own mother and brothers and sisters, and the female friends and relatives of their mother and their children. The scene for this is their own home, the adjoining back street, or the homes of their mother's friends.

The back street right outside the home is the most desirable playground to most children. There is space to run around and they may scream and shout as much as they like. But I have mentioned above that some mothers categorically refuse to allow their children to use the street as a playground (and mix with the 'street mob'): they constantly condemn the disgusting and shameless behaviour of the children in the street (*ilqaraf wa'lqillit iladab bituçhum*). Thus, they encourage the children to keep aloof from the area in which they live, look upon themselves as different and better, and develop contempt for the life patterns which distinguish the neighbourhood.

Other mothers try with less ardour to limit the children's play to the flat: they are often less concerned with the bad manners the children may learn than with the danger of rows with the neighbours. Others again see playing in the street as a bad thing, but only one of many bad things connected with poverty, to which one might as well resign oneself. Of the children playing in the street, some, however, are constantly forbidden to play with certain others due to enmity between their respective families.

The children in the street have no type of gang formation. It never happens that children from the same street get together in groups to confront another street-group. They have no leaders. Children can play together in groups of eight to ten, but if two quarrel or fight, their respective mothers rush to their defence, whereas the playmates remain passive. As far as I have seen, children are seldom or never left to sort out their differences between themselves. The mothers insist on defining them as *their* differences. If a child hits, or even unintentionally, while playing, pushes another child, its *mother* is held responsible: she has not brought up her child properly. The extreme identification of mothers with their children and their defence of them are analogous with the attitude: 'Right or wrong, *my* country'.[1] Children never go to the nearby streets to play. I see the reason as being fear

---

[1] This is systematically the opposite of conditions in Ammar's country village: 'Another important social norm reflected in play procedures is the respect shown to the leaders in directing the games, and the power enjoyed by them. They settle the disputes and smooth misunderstandings that occur during the game (p.157).

of finding themselves without the mother's support in case of conflict. As I have already shown, social relations in this neighbourhood are distinguished by frequent, strong, and long-lasting conflicts between households which constantly erupt in vehement and partly violent confrontations.

In such conflicts children are especially exposed to attack or revenge, because any aggression against them can easily be legitimized. Adults may accuse a child of having spat, put his tongue out, used foul language, or been rude and nasty as an excuse to give him a good hiding. They may do the deed themselves or send a stronger child to fight the enemy. The reverse can also happen, so that the legitimization is fabricated in retrospect. I observed one occasion which was typical in spite of being unique: after several weeks of acute conflict between two neighbouring families, A and B, A's ten-year-old daughter spat on B's daughter of the same age, as she came home to an empty house to feed the chickens. (Her mother has a little shop where the girl usually spends her days.) The girl B replied with a conventional shower of abuse, whereupon the whole crowd of enemies, adults and children, threw themselves at her, tore her hair, hit her head against the ground and bit her severely in the arm. This attracted as usual a crowd of people, great commotion resulted as well as a counter-attack from the B family, which included reporting A to the police. But the woman A who was responsible for the attack told the crowd that she would glady pay £100 for the pleasure of spoiling the girl's *'wishsh'* – face/honour. (If there is a physical injury *both* conflicting parties have to pay £5.05. If there is a confrontation without physical injury each pays £1.01.) On another typical occasion, a mother sent three of her children against the seven-year-old son of her main female enemy whilst herself cheering them on to beat him up, shouting: 'Don't let him go before you've rolled him in the mud!'

Children not only experience being falsely blamed for deeds they have not done, but are also made scapegoats for the passing on of information to which the adults will not admit. The standard phrase is: 'Don't suspect X, it was her child (or Y's child) who told me . . . ' Children can also be used by their own family as pawns in

'Their own problems must be kept to themselves and not communicated whenever possible to their adults, who are not expected to enquire about children's activities (p. 128).

'On being punished or rebuked by his elders, the child is expected to obey, while if he shows any submissiveness, if wronged by his "pals", he would be punished by his parents and would be asked to retaliate for himself' (p. 129).

the game against family enemies. It is a well-known strategy for conflicting adults to threaten to hurt themselves and then report the enemy to the police as having caused the injury. Children may be used in an analogous fashion. Mothers and elder sisters or brothers (I've never seen fathers do it) may hold little children dangling from the balcony, threatening to drop the child and then report the enemy to the police for having done it unless the enemy agrees to certain concessions. It is difficult to think of a more undeniable way of demonstrating to children how it is possible to abuse other people.

It is reasonable to suggest that the experiences gained by the children in this manner must contribute strongly to teaching them mistrust in people generally. They learn that they are not in control of their own situation, because other people can manipulate them. Regardless of what they say or do, others can punish them for made-up deeds or words. They are nothing but pawns in a game played by more powerful people.

The home, their own and that of others, is the scene of the childrens' other activities. As mentioned above, children often go visiting with their mother or are present when she receives visitors in her own home. We have seen how common it is for the women to criticize their husbands as well as men generally on such occasions. It is certain that children overhear and understand part of this, but it is difficult to tell what effect it has on them, apart from the general knowledge that 'women always criticize men for being irresponsible and selfish'. But the mother will also tell them directly similar things about their father: what kind of person he is, what he ought to be, and this partly occurs in contexts which are extremely important to the children themselves, where the mother's attitudes contrast starkly with those of the father. Thus, for instance when the family is short of money for food, clothes, school-books, school-fees, medicine, etc. it is always the mother who is immediately prepared to try her utmost to solve the problem. She communicates a consideration for the children and a solidarity for the family as a unit, which the children could never doubt. Among other things, it is always she who is prepared to try to borrow money in an emergency – although borrowing is a shameful act.

The father, on the contrary, according to the mother, is only prepared to borrow money when he himself needs it – and rarely if ever for the sake of the family. He has no concern for or understanding of them or their needs – whether they are ill, how they are doing at school or what they need in material terms. Instead it is obvious to the children that their mother places their needs above

Some of the children's social experiences whilst growing up 69

her own: she may need clothes for herself but buys for them; she may be ill and in need of a doctor but will not spend the money needed by the children; she will sell the belongings she can do without to help them. And what is more, not only does she struggle to satisfy their immediate needs but she is also concerned with planning and economizing with a view to the children's future. It is she who is mainly or solely interested in giving them an education. The father, on the contrary, complains about the extra expense brought on by schooling, and sometimes threatens to take the children away from school. Meanwhile, she saves from her housekeeping money to give them this one chance to improve their social position. Children in the first form of the elementary school seem to be already influenced by their mother's pronounced education orientation. As a seven-year-old child put it: 'I'm glad I go to school so that I can make money.'

The father's presence influences the atmosphere in the home. He is entitled to respect from the children, expressed by certain actions, such as: (i) sons must not cross their legs in front of him, and daughters must not extend their legs or fold them under; (ii) sons must not smoke in front of him, unless he himself encourages them. The children also have to show him formal respect. This implies that no intimate confidences between mother and children should be exchanged in his presence. On the basis of my direct observation and the statements of different children, I think the main features of the children's experience of their father's presence in the home are as follows: he is often tired and irritable, gets angry for no good reason, and punishes them severely. The following episode, although an isolated case, illustrates a typical aspect of the relationship between father and children. A family sat on the floor around the table, eating. Due to the lack of space they were crowded together. The mother had a one-year-old child on her lap. When the father put his glass of water to his mouth, the child waved its arms so that he dropped the glass and it was smashed. Furious, the father started to hit the child, screaming: 'I'll kill you, you daughter of a whore! Do you think I'm rolling in money?'

Interaction between mother and father largely centres on the issue of money. Quarrels about money, which the children, in such crowded quarters, cannot fail to hear, are endemic. The father often dismisses his wife's begging for money as nagging or worse, shouts at her for being demanding, uneconomical, wasteful, etc. If he learns that she has borrowed money, or if she threatens to do so, he can be overcome by rage because she does not realize that she can and must make do with what he gives her. The mother will defend herself by referring to the needs of the children, which will provoke accusations from him that she is weak and lax. He may also lose control and hit her, to the great despair of the children. (Once I was present when a five-year-old came in to see the neighbours, crying because the father had threatened: 'When your mother comes home and I hit her, you had better not cry!') But this kind of measure becomes rarer as the children grow older. The father feels he may lose esteem and all support if he behaves like that.

The positive contributions which flow from the father to the children are less evident to them. Where material values are concerned, I think, for example, that the children notice what the father *does not* give them rather than what he does give. The father is the family's formal, authoritative spokesman towards the rest of the world and always defends them in confrontations. But because of his absence from the home, he is usually not at hand when conflicts break out and can only take action later when he is given an account of the event. The mother, however, is always near and so can come to the immediate rescue of the children. I think this fact is very important for the understanding of the value the children attach to their mother versus father as protectors.

Apart from this, the father's role is limited to playing with the children when he is in the mood, and this always seems to be a great treat for them. He also on rare occasions will take children away with him into town or to visit his relatives but I do not know how much this means to the children.

In general, the children's experience of their father seems to be that he fails them but is demanding and punitive. This idea is shared by both seven-year-olds and adult men. In my material I have no instance where a child has supported its father in a conflict between the parents. Among the other families I know, I only know of one single such case. This involved a twenty-year-old boy who was exempted from military service due to his father's intervention and immediately shifted his loyalty from father to mother! On the other hand, it is common to hear children criticize their father in harsh words, chiefly when he himself is not present. During a marital conflict where the mother threatened to go away for good, the six children, aged from five to twenty-two, were unanimous that they wanted the father to go instead. 'He gives us nothing, only scolds and demands and tells us off.' The way men fulfil their paternal obligations naturally varies greatly. These variations reflect difference of character, financial ability, and priority of values. Amongst the fourteen men in the study, two fathers, Mustafa and Ibrahim, stand out as having very good relationships

Some of the children's social experiences whilst growing up 71

with their children. They are both about thirty and the oldest child is six. They also stand out for other reasons: they express clearly formulated, explicit aspirations on behalf of the family as a unit, and systematically try to realize these (see p. 151). They have chosen not to spend money on cigarettes, and are the only non-smoking men in my study. Both take an active interest in the upbringing and education of their children and are, uniquely in my sample, consistently loyal to their wives. Mustafa formulates a programme, saying he wants to be like a brother to his son so that their relationship can be trusting and close.

This to him is in extreme contrast to the relationship he has with his own father: 'I am like a slave in his house, and that's how he wants it. He begrudges me an education because he himself is illiterate. He is afraid I might raise my status, because he wants me to need him all my life.' Ibrahim can be characterized in contrast to his own half-brother who also has a six-year-old daughter. The two little girls were to start school in August 1962. On the same day that Ibrahim went out to buy shoes and a school-bag for his daughter to prepare her, his half-brother tore up his daughter's birth certificate in front of her eyes, just to show her once and for all that he did *not* have the money to send her to school.

In the relationship between fathers and adult children, a clear and consistent pattern emerges. An adult seeks to avoid any contact with his father and the fathers of adult sons express great bitterness over the lack of respect shown to them. A couple of young men I know did not even invite their fathers to their own weddings. For adult women, however, a father can be useful as a mediator or defender, but the frequency of contacts varies strongly. Some see their father living nearby a couple of times a week, others no more than perhaps every other month. But for both sexes the quality of the relationship with their father contrasts as sharply as can be with that with the mother. Throughout life the father stands out as the demanding parent and the mother as the loving one.

A child's relationship to its father must, for purely structural reasons, have the character of an enforced, one-sided dependence. The relations with brothers and sisters, however, are primarily a case of enforced proximity. The quality and intensity of the bond will be determined by variables such as sex, age, and character.

According to Egyptian culture, the elder brother has authority over the younger ones and should protect the honour of younger sisters. Elder sisters have authority over younger ones. Also, from puberty to marriage, women need an escort in many situations to be able to move freely, and this is where sisters can be of help to each other. They can also have a confidential relationship like no others within the family, and a similar relationship may exist between elder sisters and younger brothers.

However, their life situation is one where lack of space and resources force them into competition, and cripples their opportunities for self-expression: they are crowded together in the same small room, share the same bed, have their clothes packed and stowed into the same basket or cupboard – sometimes they even share clothes, and have to fight for a turn to wear them. Such conditions inevitably lead to friction. Relations between siblings are strongly affected by jealousy and are constantly charged with conflict and fighting over scant resources.[1] Amongst older siblings there are often violent outbursts where they tear up each other's valuables, such as bags, shirts, and blouses, etc., brothers may hit each other with pitchers, or threaten each other with knives. As a dominant pattern, each child is individually closely attached to the mother, whereas the relationships with brothes or sisters are quite secondary. The actual relationships between adult siblings are a direct sequel to this: in the case of adult brothers it leads to hardly any contact between them; in my sample there is not one adult man who regularly sees his brother.

The intense solidarity between mother and child, and the relative lack of intimacy between father and child are reflected by the stronger feelings for the mother's relatives as opposed to those of the father. The relatives the children see and get to know are almost exclusively from the mother's family. If their maternal grandmother is alive, the children will probably see her every day. Maternal aunts and uncles are other important relatives. The father's family, on the other hand, will rarely or never come to the house and the children go to them only occasionally. Where paternal grandmothers are concerned, it is true as the saying goes that each woman loves her daughter's children and vice versa, but she does not love her son's children, because they love their maternal grandmother.

The expected quality in the relationship between the paternal grandmother and the grandchildren can be illustrated by the following episode. A mother sent her seven-year-old son to his grandmother, asking to borrow 5p so that she could take her sick baby daughter to the doctor. The boy returned with the following message: 'I haven't got the money. And besides, Nora will only grow up to be like her mother!' (*Mamçish wa Nora hatitlaç zayy*

---

[1]See Ammar, especially pp. 166, 54, and 107 ff.

ummaha). The children learn that they can always trust their maternal grandmother and in emergencies there is always the chance that one or more of their mother's relatives will help. All one can expect from the father's relatives, however, are demands and trouble. It may even happen that the father takes their side against the children and the mother in a conflict. On the other hand, it is the father's family that will assume the burden of supporting them financially if the father dies.

Let me summarize the most important general features of this description. The nuclear family is not only an economic unit, it is also a corporation in the sense that its members share in a common fund of honour, and join together in confrontations with outsiders. But in their interactions within the family, they are constantly divided because their life situation is such that members of the family recurrently fail in their mutual obligations and quarrel over scarce resources. This leads to constant confrontations, which undermine the loyalty. The children gain a thorough knowledge of the parents' disloyalty to each other, because of the overcrowding and their parents' use of them as pawns in their own game. They will not develop any solidarity or group identity as brothers and sisters, and yet the lack of space forces them into close proximity – a closeness which must result in strife. The family consequently cannot serve them as a model of the corporation as a compelling and reliable unit of solidarity. Neither can the group of brothers and sisters form such a unit, and the small group of mother and children disintegrates because of the rivalry between the children for the love and support of the mother. The only stable relationship of trust into which the child is socialized is, consequently, the mother-child pair.

The unconditional character of this corporation is made explicit by the naming customs: as soon as a woman gives birth to a child she is addressed and referred to as 'the mother of –' (*Umm* –). Only her husband and parents and elder siblings are entitled to use her own name. The strong identification with each child is expressed by the fact that a mother can be paralyzed with grief if she loses one of her many children. Out of six women in the sample, two have had such reactions. They literally spent several years sitting immobile staring into the room, and could only be made to function again by *zar*, that is, exorcism. Another aspect of this identification is revealed when we see that the phrase 'the kids fought' seems to be regarded as the most logical and ultimate legitimate reason for any conflicts between the mothers. It is likewise striking how every mother boasts about her children with obvious conviction, seeing them as the most clever and beautiful, and insisting that others should confirm this evaluation. The basic quality of the mother's relationship to her child is usually expressed as *ilumm haniyyina* – 'the mother is loving'. A contrast to the father seems always to be implied. This concept of 'tender, loving' is also occasionally used by men to characterize their own attitude to a sister or mother, but I have never heard a father described in those terms. Throughout a person's life the mother in fact continues to be the only stable source of the essential values of love, security, and support. The following episode reveals this most clearly. Umm Hussein wanted to go to Alexandria to see her father, her only close relation. Her husband refused to let her and a female spectator supported him: 'What in Heaven's name do you want to go there for, you haven't even got a mother!' As the children grow up, the mother is also experienced as a source or perhaps as *the* source of material values, because she often succeeds in providing what the father is obliged but fails to give, and because the contributions that originate from him only reach them *through* her.

The prototypical learning situation sketched here will be somewhat or radically changed if the parents die or are divorced, which frequently happens among these people. In my material I know that at least fifteen out of the thirty-one married persons have had such childhood experiences. I have only incomplete data about this for some of the men. Which parent they lose makes an enormous difference for the children.

Let me first deal with the consequences of losing a mother. This can be due either to death or divorce. A father has the legal right to his children after a son is seven and a daughter nine. It is very likely that a divorced man or a widower will remarry soon, which means the children will have a stepmother. She could never replace a mother, because each woman concentrates her interest and love on her own children and any other children will come second. It is natural and obvious, judging from the empirical material, that she regards the stepchildren as a threat to the resources which are already too scant for her own children. The stereotype image of the relation stepmother-stepchildren is that the stepmother hates her stepchildren, the sole reason for this being seen as the battle over money. The poor therefore express their amazement that the same quality seems to pervade this relationship among the rich (information they gain from television plays) where there should be no reasons for such feelings.

With this conception of intrinsic enmity in the relationship between stepmother and stepchildren go a set of clear, stereotyped

Some of the children's social experiences whilst growing up 75

expectations about role performance in the relationship. The stepmother keeps lying about the stepchildren to their father, claims that they are rude, obstinate, and disobedient, in an attempt to set him against them (*taslit*). And in accordance with the folk generalization that the man does as the wife says (*irrágil biyismaç kalám mirátu*), she is expected to succeed: the father will constantly punish the children severely and drastically reduce their share of material goods. One childhood memory shows the realities of such a situation: 'Once father came home, took off his shoe and hit it against my head. I cried so desperately that the neighbours came rushing to intervene. Meanwhile, father's wife stood, arms akimbo, enjoying the scene. "That's how it should be. She gets what she deserves." Today I can't take any pressure against the back of my head because of that rough treatment.'

This is what a child will expect from its stepmother, and since there is a fundamental suspicion about all people, which can only be eliminated by a person being *only* good always, the chances are overwhelming that every stepmother will confirm these role expectations (I know of only one case where a child had a different experience. That stepmother is a highly religious woman who has made pilgrimages to Mecca and seems to try practising her religion in social relations generally. Both her present and her former husbands were relatively well-off.) Stepchildren therefore grow up without belonging to any group, unless there is an older sister who can partly replace the mother.

The self-fulfilling character of the stepmother stereotype can be exemplified by the following event. A woman had brought up a stepdaughter for seventeen years when the daughter suddenly died, at the age of twenty. People's talk (*kal ám innás*) had it that the stepmother had killed her by poisoning. The woman learnt about the gossip and had a post mortem carried out in order to clear herself. The doctor's authoritative verdict was that the girl had died from natural causes. The popular talk then concluded that the woman had bribed the doctor with £5 for the verdict. Even now – five years later – the accusations about murder stick.

The loss of a father has a far less drastic effect on the socialization of a child. Widows often try to remain single and provide for themselves and the children out of consideration for them. Everybody knows that a man will either strongly dislike or refuse to provide for stepchildren. Some women manage to bring up their children alone but most remarry after a while. I have no first-hand information about the manner in which such a new family situation will affect her children, but the folk generalization is: 'A mother favours the children she has with her living husband.' (*Ilumm bithibb awlādha min gozha illi maçaha aktar.*) I also know of two instances where a mother sent her children away because after a while her new husband refused to keep them. In one case the children were placed with their paternal uncle, and his wife lived up to all the expectations of a stepmother; in the other case the children grew up with their maternal grandmother who became a satisfactory replacement for the mother — in full accordance with expectations.

In order to illustrate some of the central themes in this chapter (and also the previous one) I will conclude with a long, detailed case history. This uncovers the roles and ambivalent attitudes and feelings of family members in an exceptionally dramatic situation. Concretely, it may serve as an illustration of sibling rivalry, the children's attitude to and experience of father versus mother, and the parents' respective attitudes to their children, and to the task of child rearing.

These events took place on the last day of Ramadan in 1969. Ramadan is the fast month of the Moslems. It is terminated by a three-day celebration which can be compared to our Christmas. But because, just like Christmas, it calls for great expense, the feast turns to sorrow in many poor homes. And the month of Ramadan, which is supposed to be the time for peace and reconciliation, instead often turns into a month of discord, with dramatic manifestations of all manner of interhuman conflict and strife. In the words of the poor themselves at the end of the festivities: 'Praise be to God it's over! During this month and the one preceding people are so angry and irritable, for Ramadan brings so many expenses, and wages which are not normally enough even for food must cover food, baking, clothes, and gifts this month.' In Cairo the clothes are definitely the most important thing, since children cannot take part in the festivities without new, colourful ones. If someone tries, he or she will immediately be scorned and sneered at by the other children. This is considered very shameful.

The family where this conflict took place is the most prosperous of the seventeen in the sample. The father has an income of about twice the average. The family has nine children aged between four and twenty-four (1969).

The eldest son, Gamal, (twenty-four) has been pressing his father for days for a new sweater for Ramadan. The father has rejected his demands, saying that he does *not* have the money. Gamal is furious, shouts and screams, and takes it out on his brothers and sisters. They are desperate but cannot retaliate, since Gamal

Some of the children's social experiences whilst growing up

is the eldest and therefore has a right to command them. And who can draw the line between rightful exertion of authority and abuse of power?

I went to see the family on several occasions during those days, and each time Gamal's mother and eldest sister Laila (twenty-two) expressed their despair:

> 'Gamal is horrible. He only thinks of himself and his friends, whereas he curses his brothers and sisters. All he ever does is demand things for himself, he can't stand it if one of the others get something. He has *masses* of clothes: a suit and three pairs of trousers and three or four shirts and he wears out one pair of shoes every three months. But in spite of that he wants new clothes for Ramadan this year "I shall have it," he says – and the whole house has to suffer for his temper.'

> 'But I feel really sorry for Hamdi [brother of twenty], and for myself [Laila] He doesn't have a sweater or even a shirt with long sleeves. He has no shoes and has to walk around in rubber sandals. Still, he says nothing, because he knows that Dad can't afford to buy anything. If he could, he would have given us things. Daddy is desperate because he can't give us children what he knows we need. A few days ago Hamdi asked Dad for a sweater and Dad said: "I can't afford it." But he has promised Hamdi a long-sleeved shirt instead. It won't keep him warm, but Hamdi is grateful anyway. That should have been Gamal!'

> 'Gamal only loves himself. Each day Mummy gives him 10p for pocket-money. During Ramadan she asked him to make do with only 5p a day and contribute to the more expensive food with the rest but he wouldn't hear of it. If he can't have his own way, he takes it out on his mother and brothers and sisters, shouts and screams and makes life unbearable for us. Hamdi on the other hand gives Mummy almost all of the 40p he gets on the days when he works.'

On the last day of Ramadan I went to their home at about five in the afternoon, only fifteen minutes after gunfire had proclaimed the end of the fast. The father and Hamdi sat watching television in one room whilst the mother, Gamal, Laila, and the other brothers and sisters sat in the other. They all looked sad and the mother was crying. I sat down with the women and they gave me this account of the scene.

Half an hour earlier, while the Koran recital about peace and reconciliation among people was being read out on the radio, the father sat listening with his two elder sons Gamal and Hamdi.

Suddenly Gamal burst out: 'Aren't you going to give me that sweater? I *shall* have it!'

Hamdi: 'In that case I want one too. I have nothing, I have to go out wearing pyjamas, but you have both suit, shirt, and sweater.'

Gamal: 'Shut up you . . .'

Hamdi, unperturbed: 'And where will Dad get the money? Instead of just demanding all the time, you should go out and make some money yourself! I wish you would be called up for the war with Israel so that all these demands of yours could end!'

This made Gamal explode: 'Shut up, I'm better than you, you illiterate, you queer!'

He took the sofa cushion and started to hit Hamdi with it. Hamdi took another and hit back. Gamal rushed into the kitchen, grabbed a knife and tried to stab his brother. Hamdi ran out and found another knife, while the mother intervened. Gamal hit a glass with his knife so that it fell to the floor and broke.

The father shouted, furious: 'Get out of my house, go away! I have brought you up until now, this is enough. Go out and provide for yourself, get yourself a job like your brother!' Gamal replied by walking out of the room into the room next door.

Then the father attacked his wife: 'It's *your* fault because you gave the £2 to Mona and promised Gamal a sweater. [Mona is a daughter of sixteen. She has a girl-friend whose mother sells sweaters cheaply. The mother has given Mona £2 as down payment for a sweater for Gamal.] You're incapable of bringing up my children. From now on my orders are to be followed, and only mine, do you hear?

'You have ruined my children completely. It's not possible for a father to hold back on the one side while the mother gives from the other. Then she sets the children up against their father, by giving them the impression that he is selfish and inconsiderate. One day they will hate me and despise my commands, and I shall no longer be master in my own house!

'That's why you *have to* stand beside me and support my authority. I'm trying to get you to understand how our household should be run: We must keep accounts and make do with my wages so that we don't have to borrow money — so that we can make a fresh start each month. With your ways of borrowing here and there just as it suits you, without a thought for planning ahead or keeping accounts, we are always in debt.

'. . . You say it's none of my business that you borrow money because you pay it back from the £35 I give you each month as housekeeping money. Are you so stupid that you don't realize that *I* am the one who has to pay even if *you* borrow and save?'

Laila and the mother were furious with the father and supported Gamal, although only a couple of days before they condemned his behaviour and blamed him for being too demanding and thinking only of himself. Now they changed their tune:

'Of course Gamal should have a new sweater considering the higher status of his friends. He rubs shoulders with officers and doctors. He would be disgraced if he didn't have a new sweater for the festivities, because friends are made here not by character but by your financial status, as it appears to others. No one at the university will want to be his friend unless he has a new sweater. But Hamdi doesn't need a sweater, because he has no friends and never goes out. It's mean of Hamdi not to let Gamal have his sweater.'

I reminded them of the statements they had made only the other day, but all they said to that was that sweaters were fashionable and therefore Gamal *must* have one. (Gamal, in the meantime, had promised Laila that he would bring her a suitor, one of his friends. It's very likely that this favour had earned him the support of both the mother and Laila. They were both unhappy because Laila is an 'old maid'.) Laila kept complaining about her father:

'He doesn't want to give us anything – he only thinks of himself, buys himself everything and borrows if he hasn't got the money. But he won't lift a finger for us.' (It is, for example, the mother who keeps Gamal in a technical college by saving from her housekeeping money. The father refuses to contribute.) 'Every single year we spend Ramadan sitting inside crying hardly daring to look from behind the curtains at the merrymakers, for fear they might see us and ask us to come out. It would be such a shame to show that we haven't got the clothes.'

She chose to demonstrate the extent of her father's meanness with the following story. Once the father bought her two golden bracelets for £35 out of the £50 he had got from a saving club. 'The better dressed a nubile girl is, and the more gold she wears, the better are her chances of a good marriage.' (Her father appeared and supported this statement.) I asked why. 'Because people, if they see her and her family walking around badly dressed, will fear that the father might put the bride-price into his own pocket and give her a miserable dowry. The shoes are particularly important. For example, when people are waiting at the bus stop, they are all busy glancing critically at each other's shoes.'

When people saw her bracelets they said that the father would soon take them back because he would need the money. He has a reputation for borrowing a lot. Laila was so happy with her bracelets. 'I beamed with joy each time I looked at them, and I gained weight and my cheeks became redder and I was beautiful. I threatened to set fire to myself if anyone took them away from me.' About a month later the sinister forecast was realized; the father wanted the bracelets. For a long time after, she cried each time she looked at her bare arm . . . .

The mother comforted Gamal, saying that she would try and borrow money for his sweater. She also theatened that she would not come home the next day (she was on her way to the cemetery in order to spend the night there, according to tradition) but celebrate away from home. Laila cried: '*Wa law magatísh – enti ḥurr!*' ('And if you don't come home, you'll have to take the responsibility yourself!')

In the end they did not get any of the new clothes they had hoped for: shoes and a handbag for Laila, a handbag and shoes for Mona, sweaters for the younger brothers, shoes and sweaters for the younger sisters, sweaters for Gamal and Hamdi. Laila just kept crying. She had been so sure she would get something new for Ramadan this year in return for all the work she does at home for nothing. Yesterday she could not control herself anymore but shouted at her father: 'I'm treated like a hired help!'

This was the eve of the festivities. I left the house at about eight o'clock and returned at about ten-thirty. I then found all the children asleep in one bed. The father had just gone out. The next morning I went back to see them. All the children were indoors, standing by the window looking at the happy children in new clothes outside. There was a mood of resignation. They were used to being spectators.

SIX
Intrigue-spinning and the forming of alliances surrounding betrothal

The conventions surrounding courtship and marriage are changing in the direction of granting the woman greater freedom of choice, and giving the couple increased opportunity to get to know each other before the wedding. Adult women express the view that many problems in their own marriages are partly due to the fact that their husbands were chosen for them, not by them. All the women in the study, except two, had no influence at all or just nominal influence on the choice of husband. Some met their fiancé a few times during the period of engagement, others not until the wedding day. Thinking of their own experiences the women express a firm wish for their own daughters to get a better start in life. For this reason, contemporary material dealing with the arranging of marriage cannot be used directly to illustrate the background of the adult women. But it does show fundamental features of the social organization of the back streets: (i) how other people, to a large extent, determine what happens between the couples during the period of engagement and thus affect their future marriage; (ii) how the quality of interpersonal relations are affected by self-fulfilling folk generalizations; it will also be shown clearly (iii) how larger kin groups play an insignificant role in social life, contrary to the general Western idea of life in the Middle East; and (iv) what difference the current changes in conventions may bring to the chances of success in marriage.

The arranging of marriage is not a transaction between two family corporations. This is in sharp contrast to the practice in most other Arabic countries where each marriage is the common concern of a group of relatives on both the man's and the woman's side. Among poor people in Cairo, however, the bridegroom acts as an independent individual towards the family of the bride, represented by her guardian and/or mother. Marriage does not establish any mutual obligations between the families of the bridegroom and bride, it is seen as an agreement between husband and wife, and as an absolutely vital step for both man and woman, to enable them to realize themselves personally. Neither does marriage entail any obligations between the person and his/her in-laws. Formally, a woman should certainly obey and serve her husband's mother and sister, but few people expect that ideal to be fulfilled. A husband obtains exclusive rights regarding his wife, and can even refuse to let her see her parents. Marriage, in other words, established a first priority obligation between two people, each of whom is also tied to blood relations by legal and/or strong moral obligations.

The process of courtship and marriage is a lengthy one. There are five formal stages. The whole process usually stretches over two to three years. One year is seen as the minimum.

The different stages are as follows:

(1) *Ittifaq* = agreement between the bridegroom and the bride's guardian with a specification of the bride-price (*mahr*), the bride's engagement present (*shabka* – gold jewellery) and the bride's dowry (*qafsh*). The bride-price and the engagement present are specified in money, the dowry as the number of rooms for which the bride has to bring furniture. The proposal as such is presented by a spokesman, reportedly so that a possible rejection does not have to be taken by the bridegroom personally, and he can cover up for it by blaming the spokesman for not performing his task properly and try again. Unlike many other Middle East countries, the suitor does not need a spokesman to emphasize his many positive characteristics. Self-praise is quite acceptable and expected in social relations generally. It was for example the most natural thing for a man to ask me whom I thought was the more beautiful in a wedding photo he showed me – himself or the bridegroom?

(2) *Fatha* = the opening verse in the Koran is read in the bride's home a short time (a couple of days to a week) after the agreement. This is the first official statement of the agreement. A few friends or relatives of either party may be present, usually the bride's mother's closest women-friends and one or two of her relations and two to four friends of the bridegroom.

After *Fatha* the bridegroom can go to the bride's home whenever he likes, and in most cases he takes great advantage of this freedom. Part of the time he will sit together with the bride, her mother, and possible visitors, mainly women, for the rest of the time the young couple will be given a chance to sit together alone, talking. *Fatha* gives the bridegroom the right to decide about the girl's way

Alliances surrounding betrothal 83

of dressing e.g., whether she may wear lipstick, cut her hair, wear her dresses short, etc. It is not generally accepted that the couple go out together (in the company of others) after *Fatḥa*, but some do.

(3) *Shabka* = engagement. The bridegroom gives the bride golden bracelets (about one to ten, the most common here being two to four), a ring, and possibly also earrings. The bride's family gives a party and the bride's father and the bridegroom share the expenses. This takes place mainly in the street where chairs are placed and a section is lit by coloured lights. The women, almost without exception, stay indoors, and relatively few accept the food and drink that are offered. In the street there is music and a crowd of uninvited children from the neighbourhood as well as the male guests. (At celebrations, women and men are always segregated.) The young couple have their photograph taken indoors. The host and hostess gain prestige by having many guests and therefore the pattern is here as in the following two stages, to invite all and sundry, even enemies. Many of the people invited will fail to appear, including many close relations. The composition of the guests can in fact only be determined by a knowledge of the current friendships and enmities of the bride's family and the bridegroom's. The closest friends and relations of the young couple are expected to bring little gifts, such as cakes or money. After the engagement it is generally accepted that the couple go out together in the company of a relative.

(4) *Katb'ikkitāb* = The marriage contract is signed by the bridegroom, the bride's guardian, and the bride herself in the presence of a Muslim dignitary and witnesses. The couple are now officially married. The marriage contract contains a specification of the bride-price and the *muaxxar issudaq* – the amount payable to the woman in case of divorce (usually half of the bride-price). The celebration is held at the home of the bride or the bridegroom. The bridegroom pays all expenses in connection with it, including dress, shoes, handbag, and hairdressing for the bride. The newly-weds are still not allowed to go out together, but may go out with an escort. It may happen that *Katb'ikkitāb* and also the next stage take place secretly in the presence of only a trusted group of friends, the reason being fear that envious people might create trouble or even destroy the ceremony (a spurned suitor for example, or the family of a girl who had hoped for the bridegroom to marry her). Another expressed reason given for such secrecy is, however, that relatives will only come to criticize and then go around saying: 'The bride was ugly, the bridegroom was ugly, the food looked awful, etc.'

(5) *Duxla* = the entry; i.e. the marriage is consummated, the bride's honour is confirmed, and the couple start living together. This ritual can assume one form out of two: 'the folk's way' (*a la baladi*) or 'French fashion' (*a la frangi*). In the first instance the bride's family will have a party (often with the cheapest kind of belly dancers as entertainment) and the bride's honour is proved, before the party is formally over, in the presence of the bridegroom and some of the bride's female relatives. The bridegroom then has to break her hymen with his forefinger. But several women tell me that the man feels so ill-at-ease in this situation that in their cases one of the female spectators had to take care of the matter and carry it out. One or several blood-stained handkerchieves are then triumphantly shown to the guests. With the 'French' method the couple go alone to a casino to celebrate, and then return to their flat alone. The next morning the bridegroom has to present a blood-stained handkerchief to the bride's family. (It seems that more and more men choose the 'French' method to avoid the embarrassing scene with the forefinger.)

Two days before the wedding itself, an important act takes place. That is when the bride's parents and the bridegroom sign a 'list' (*qaima*) of each and every item the bride will bring along in her dowry – except for clothes, linen, and breakable kitchen utensils (i.e. all perishable goods). This list is the bride's proof of her property. According to both male and female informants it is necessary to prevent the husband from being tempted to sell off his wife's property when she is absent (possibly after inventing some excuse to get her to go). Consequently, it is not so important when the bride's family are close neighbours of the couple, as they will keep an eye on the home. It is a powerful symbol of trust if the bride's family does not demand a 'list'. I know of two occasions where this happened. In one instance the lack of security had tragic consequences for the woman, as the husband 'stole' her furniture (after having encouraged her to go to the country to see relatives) and gave it as bride-price for a second wife. In the other case the wife finds her manoeuvring position in marriage greatly hampered, since she fears ever to leave the house (see p. 53) for an extended period of time.

Stages (1) and (2) are always separated in time. The other three stages can be combined freely according to wish. On most occasions stages (2) and (4) are connected, or (3) and (4) are. The main reason for variations of timing is the problem of getting the bride-price or the dowry together. Getting married is an expensive process. The bride-price varies between £50 and £150 and this sum normally has to be earned by the bridegroom himself. The bride's parents on their side have to provide their daughter with a dowry which should be three or four times the size of the bride-price. In other words, the more the bridegroom can pay, the more he can demand. The size of the bride-price and the proportional dowry is a public measure of the status of the bride's family and, just as much, of the bridegroom (for example, one woman quarrelling with another: 'You came as bride with only a handbag, I came with furniture and money!' (*Enti daxalti bi shánta bass, iḥna daxalna bi qáfsh wa fulús!*)) Moreover, for the rest of her life the bride will regard the dowry she had as a measurement of her parents' appreciation of her.

However, depending on how strongly one party desires the other, these general expectations can be set aside. A bridegroom can be prepared to forsake the dowry, or the bride's family may pay everything and the groom nothing – but if so this *must* be concealed from the public (see p. 145). If neither bride nor groom has any money they may get married with a minimum of furniture (and fake rings and jewellery) and then save together and buy things on hire purchase.

Where the formally agreed dowry is concerned, I doubt that it is fulfilled on most occasions. The data about household budgets indicate that it would take very long indeed to save anything like such sums, and it is quite likely that the bridegroom becomes impatient to consummate the marriage and therefore agrees to accept (sometimes considerably) less: an old cupboard instead of a nice new one, two mattresses instead of three, etc.

One conspicuous feature of courtship and marriage in this community is how it intensifies old conflicts and creates new ones. This happens both because many people have parallel and competing interests in boys and girls as marriage partners, and because the marriage negotiations in themselves create a battleground where other conflicts can also be played out.

The greatest difficulties regarding the conventional expectations inhere in the relationship mother-in-law/daughter-in-law. As we have seen, this relationship is rife with competition for money as well as with emotional rivalry. As one woman put it: 'The son used to give his mother money and sleep in her house. Now she fears he will cease doing both.' (See informant's statement in Ammar (1954) p. 51: 'The husband's mother is resentful of the fact that her son's attachment, which was solely hers before marriage, is shared with his wife.')

Apart from a series of different accounts of the marriage process, I have direct observational material from six different sequences.

Three of these broke up after stage (2); one has reached stage (2) and is being attacked from the outside (later I learnt that this, too, was broken after stage (2)); one has passed stage (1) and is threatened by breach, and one has passed stage (4).

The empirical material concerning marriage establishment is best given in accounts of a few detailed instances. I shall here relate two such cases to exemplify the hopes of the various parties, their expectations and actions in a relevant context.

The main character is Laila, twenty-four years old (1972) – an unusually high age for an unmarried woman. Her parents are the best-off in the sample. She herself explains her unmarried status in two ways: each time a suitor comes or plans coming to her, envious people drive him off; besides, few men ever discover her, because she has 'been sitting in the house' for twelve years – ever since she left elementary school – and because her elder brother never lets his friends see her. (He is ashamed of the flat – perhaps of his sister too – and never brings his friends home.) 'It's the girls who go to work who have the best chance of getting married, both because more men see them and because men nowadays want a woman who can make money. Only men who earn at least £30 will take a girl who doesn't work, apart from "men from the country".' Some time ago a suitor from the country came to her. She wanted to accept him, but her mother refused: 'If you fall ill or something else goes wrong with you, who will look after you?'

The following events took place during the course of four months in 1971. I relate it from her own account, although much abbreviated and edited:

'The bridegroom, Mahmoud went to the shoemaker on the ground floor asking him if he could recommend a possible bride. The shoemaker said: "There are two in this house, two sisters, one white and one black. [These colours refer to nuances of skin colour. The whiter, the better.] Come and sit in my shop tomorrow afternoon, and I'll show you when they walk past or come out on the balcony."

Mahmoud came, saw the two of us, and said about Mona [the sister]: "I don't like the black one" and about me *"That one* I'd like!" The shoemaker talked to Dad, and they agreed that Mahmoud should come to our house the following day. He came with the shoemaker, a friend, and his friend's uncle. Dad and Gamal [elder brother] received them. The shoemaker was the spokesman and said that Mahmoud wanted to pay £150 as a bride-price and £50 for engagement presents. As dowry he

View of the back street environment

One of the widest back streets

(above) One of the typical door-sitters, a poor widow, photographed in her basement room with her daughter and all their belongings

(left) The father of a family mixing rose water as an extra job in the evenings

Friends visiting

A family portrait after twenty years of marriage. Mother is thirty-three, father thirty-nine. Three children died as infants but since this picture was taken, another child has been born

A strong-willed woman, twenty years old and the mother of three, intent on establishing a position for herself in relation to her husband. (Photographed in her kitchen next to the entrance to the lavatory)

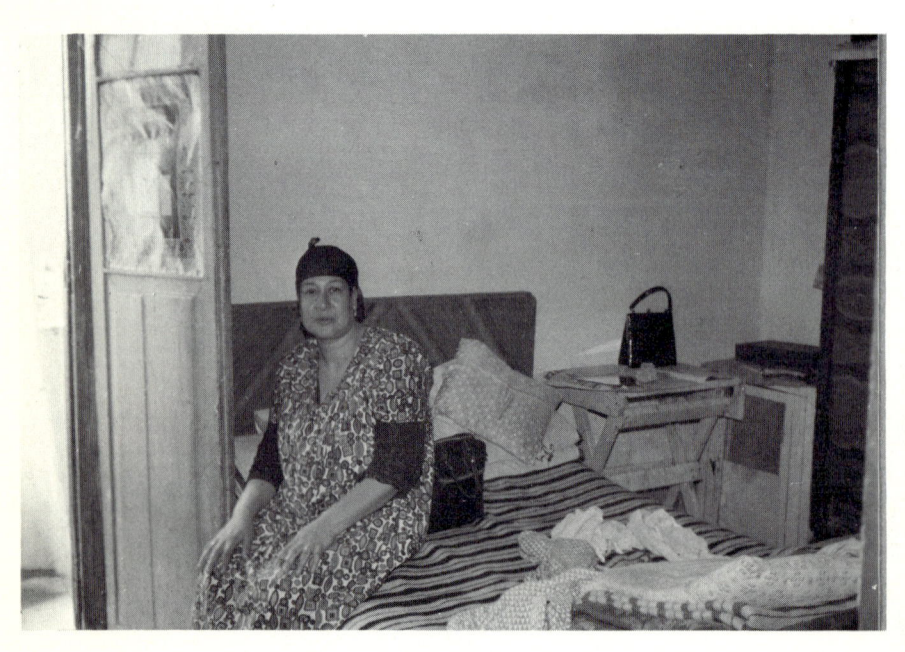

An unusually independent and domineering woman, but now resigned and tired after twenty-two years of marital drudgery. At the age of thirty-seven she has borne eight children, four of whom are now in their teens

wanted furniture for three rooms. I knew nothing of all this, I had gone out shopping. When I came back I could hear there were male visitors in the sitting-room. Mummy told me that a bridegroom had come for me. Dad came to get me and I greeted all the men. I understood which was Mahmoud from the way he looked at me. I thought he was beautiful. The men decided to read the Koran three days later.

Mahmoud wrote us a note with his name, his birthdate and address in the army and the names of the male members of his family, so that we could find out what kind of family he came from. We did the same for him. When we saw that Mahmoud was related to N.N., a prominent army officer, we did not bother to check any further.

The following day his friend's uncle, who had been present during the agreement, came to us and said we shouldn't believe that Mahmoud could pay a bride-price of £150 and buy engagement presents for £50. "He's only cheating you! All he will pay is £100 and £30."

We got upset, of course, and put off the Koran reading to find out. When we asked Mahmoud he was very upset that a man he thought was his friend had deceived him like that. *Of course* we could trust his word! Then we fixed the Koran reading for one week later.

Later we found out that this man had lied about Mahmoud because he thought I was pretty and wanted me to marry his son.

During the following weeks Mahmoud came to us every day and stayed until late at night. So did our relatives – to spy on us and get something to gossip about.

One day his sister came with him to see Mummy and discuss my dowry. Among other things Mahmoud demanded four mattresses. Mummy said that was impossible since he was only paying a bride-price of £150. They agreed on three mattresses.

I put on my green dress for the Koran reading. "Take it off immediately!" Mahmoud said when he saw me. "It's too short!" "But the other one is dirty," I said. "I must wear this one." "No question of it," Mahmoud said, and I had to put on the dirty dress. Mummy and Mustafa's wife asked him if they could make me up with rouge. He said no.

On Mahmoud's side came a brother, a sister and her husband, and two friends.

On our side came Grandad, mother's two brothers and their wives, one of mother's sisters and cousins and my brothers and sisters.[1] The evening was spoiled because Mummy's sister insulted both Mahmoud and us by saying what a pity it was that Mummy had breastfed Anwar, her son, when he was a baby, for she would have liked me to marry *him*! It was because of Zenab [Uncle's wife] that she did this. For one day the previous week when she came to see us — to watch television! she only comes in her own interest — she heard Mahmoud whisper to me: "Don't sit next to that fellow" [i.e. Anwar]. Mahmoud was jealous — quite naturally — all bridegrooms are jealous — because Anwar had slapped me on the shoulder. Zenab immediately ran to Mummy's sister to tell her, and she felt awfully insulted on behalf of her son.

The following day we expected Mahmoud to come round but he didn't. We waited for days, but he might as well have gone up in smoke. It was obvious that people were manipulating him (*nás sallaṭúh*). One day our seamstress saw him in the shop run by the wife of my dead uncle. They seemed to be having a confidential conversation. We realized something was going on. A few days later Hamdi [younger brother] met Mahmoud in the street and accused him of having deceived me. Mahmoud defended himself saying he had had to go back to the army. "That's a lie!" Hamdi said. "We have seen you with our uncle's wife. Laila never wants to see you again!" "I don't care," Mahmoud said, "she's going to marry her cousin anyway!"

To cut a long story short: the uncle's wife had manipulated Mahmoud and tried to convince him that I was getting married to her son, because she herself wanted to marry Mahmoud! Yes, it *is* true that the son wanted to marry me, but both she, he and everyone else know that I *don't* want him! He's a disgusting, unbearable type.

Hamdi explained the whole thing to Mahmoud, and three weeks after the Koran reading we were reunited. Mahmoud began to come round again regularly at night, and so did our relatives, of course. They pretended they came to watch television, but it was quite obvious that they came only to torment us. Mummy's sister said to her: "I could *see* that her knee was touching his!" And they kept fabricating lies like that. For a whole year I was not on speaking terms with Zenab because she went round saying: "Laila sits close to Mahmoud

---

[1] The following relatives who live nearby failed to appear: two of mother's sisters, one of mother's cousins on her father's side, the cousin's adult children, two of father's sisters with adult children, father's son, uncle and the children of a dead uncle.

and goes out with him regularly (alone)." When they asked me whether I loved Mahmoud, I never dared say yes, because then they would have gossiped about that. I loved Mahmoud, but it became more and more difficult to be with him, because he was so jealous. "Don't wear that nightgown, you look naked!" "Your skirt is too short!" "Don't cut your hair!" "Don't do this and don't do that!" It was other people who manipulated him and made him so overwrought. Friends went to him and said: "I saw her in the street wearing that (short) skirt you don't like." "I saw her with that bitch, you know.", etc. I was always unhappy because he tormented me so. One day he tore my dress into pieces in a rage. I was so desperate I just wanted to set fire to myself. Gamal [elder brother] told Mahmoud to go to hell. He had never liked Mahmoud, because he wanted me to marry my uncle's wife's son. They were friends then. Now they are not on speaking terms.

Mahmoud stayed away for three weeks. One day his brother went past and we called him in. He said we shouldn't bother any more with Mahmoud − our family deserve a better man than he. But Mahmoud sent a letter to me through Gamila (girl-friend) which said: "My dearest sister Laila" and that he loved me and how unhappy he was because he had hurt me. Then one night at midnight there was someone at the door − I had gone to bed. Hamdi opened. There was Mahmoud. He said he knew he shouldn't have come so late but he had been travelling all night and had come straight to us to promise to mend his ways.

So we had a new reconciliation. We were told that Mahmoud had fallen out with his brother because the brother wanted Mahmoud to sign a contract for the £150 which he had promised to lend him for the bride-price. Mahmoud refused. When his own brother expressed such mistrust he would rather borrow from a bank! Mahmoud kept coming to see us for a while. But then one day he was seen again with our uncle's wife. I was furious because I had told him to keep away from her. Then his visits became more irregular again and one day a friend of his came to Gamal and said: "Don't let yourselves be taken in by Mahmoud. He is not the marrying kind, (*huwa mish bitác iggawáz*) he's just amusing himself with girls." Then I decided I would never see Mahmoud again. He was very unhappy and tried to get some mutual friends of ours to bring us together so that he could explain, but I refused. One day Hoda [girl-friend] sent me a message to come and see her. I went − opened the door and − there was Mahmoud! I screamed and ran home. Hoda told me that Mahmoud still loved me but was also afraid of getting into trouble with my uncle's wife's son, because my uncle's wife kept threatening that her son considered he had a right to me. I asked Hoda to tell Mahmoud that he was lacking in character to believe in gossip rather than my word.

By the way, we later found out that Mummy's sister, Umm Anwar – she is base (*laîma*) – had allied herself with my uncle's wife and encouraged her to get me to marry her son, just to be popular with my uncle's wife so that she would get presents from Kuwait the next time my uncle's wife comes back! [Uncle's wife, who works in Kuwait.]

So both Mahmoud and I were unhappy. He tried to use Mona [younger sister], Hamdi [younger brother] and others to bring us together. I also had a lovely letter from him which it had taken him four days to write. I felt like seeing him, but Gamal [older brother] said no. At a birthday party of a cousin of mine I met Ibrahim, the brother of her best friend, who is a friend of Mahmoud's – they come from the same village. I told him everything that had happened and he said I'd better forget Mahmoud for good. Then he told me that Mahmoud had come to him some time ago and asked him to help him get back the £7 Mahmoud had given me two months ago to join the saving club for him. "I was cheated," Mahmoud had said. "It turned out that she had bad manners/character" (*lagēt axlaqha wisha*). Ibrahim had replied: "No, you should let her keep the money for in the country you're not even allowed to see the bride's character before the wedding." [This refers to the fact that in the country bride and groom are not even allowed to see each other before the wedding.] But I don't want to have anything from Mahmoud. He will have his money back as soon as I get it from the saving club.

Four months passed from the moment I first saw Mahmoud until we broke up, now that's a year ago. But I still love him, and he loves me. He keeps going to the shoemaker to sit there in order to catch a glimpse of me. It was *other people* who manipulated him and destroyed our relationship. I still want to marry him. But Dad says there is no question of it, because Mahmoud has proved himself a man who does not keep his word. I can never forget Mahmoud because he was the first man ever to find his way into my heart (*awwil wâḥid il xashsh fi qalbi*), he was the man who taught me about love, he aroused a yearning in my body. But actually, I would marry anyone, even one from Upper Egypt, to get away from this house and family. And it's true that it is better not to marry someone whose feet you will kiss. You should marry someone who will kiss your feet. Such a man will make a good life for you and then in due course you'll learn to love him.'

I have mentioned that the main problem in connection with marriage establishment often arises between the mother-in-law and daughter-in-law. In the previous case this was not relevant, because Mahmoud's mother was dead. I would therefore like to illustrate the dilemma with Laila's seventeen-year-old sister Mona, who had already, after passing the first stage of the negotiations, reached this situation.

She and her bridegroom Abdu, aged eighteen, had fallen in love with each other at a distance. When Abdu came to ask for her hand in marriage, he came with his older brother. Mona's father said he should have brought his mother on such an occasion since she was the head of the family (the father is dead). The brother replied that she approved of the enterprise. 'But you know what women are like ... To avoid trouble it's better to leave her out until the engagement [stage (3)].'

The agreement was entered into, and everything seemed to be all right. Abdu took Mona to her job every day so that no men would molest her on the bus. He immediately agreed to raise the formally agreed bride-price to £180 when Mona's mother decided that £150 was not enough. (£180 is the highest bride-price I have ever heard of in this neighbourhood.) He came to see them daily, sometimes with cakes for his future mother-in-law. But this happy situation lasted hardly two weeks. Then Mona's mother discovered that Abdu's mother, who always used to greet her from her kitchen window (in the house next door), now walked away instead. Something must have gone wrong. And they soon found out by way of gossip what it was: Abdu's mother did not at all approve of the marriage. Abdu had in fact already had a Koran reading with the sister of his brother's wife and the mother still wanted him to marry her. The bride's family was upset when they learnt about Abdu's mother's attitude. (The fact that Abdu had already read the Koran with someone else seemed to worry them only indirectly, probably because such broken agreements are a common pattern among these people.) 'Now she'll go round saying that we have manipulated her son and taken him away from her. People will talk and say that we have *stolen* the son from the mother and a lot of trouble and enmity will result. We can't have anything more to do with Abdu before his mother accepts the marriage.' They refused to let Abdu see Mona. He sent a long letter to her mother where he gave a reason for his behaviour, expressed his love for Mona, and threatened to kill himself if he couldn't see her. 'Let him kill himself,' said the bride's mother. 'His own mother will be guilty.'

Another issue aggravated the situation. Abdu had leave from the army but did not go back when it expired. The bride's family interpreted this as fear in him that they might promise the girl to someone else while he was away. Among other things, they 'knew' that Laila's previous suitor and others who wanted revenge on the family were gossiping actively to create this kind of mistrust in Abdu. But the real source of their despair was the simple fact that he had not left. 'Now of course people will say that *we* have manipulated him not to go. *We* will be blamed!' To the bride's family it seemed apparent that people, including Abdu's mother, would greedily seize this new theme to use against them. Abdu's mother would have a double interest in doing so: to excuse the son and to criticize them. They themselves stood open to attack, since Abdu *had not* gone.

It is unusual for the bride's family to let themselves be influenced by the bridegroom's mother in this way. It is expected that she will always be dissatisfied with her son's choice and will want to choose her daughter-in-law herself to ensure that she retains control of him, therefore the bride's family usually ignores any protests from her. The bridegroom, on the other hand will often become unsure of his own judgement in such a situation, since women are seen as the only ones who understand and can detect the hidden natures of other women. Therefore his mother and/or elder sister's judgement will often win out in the long run for his choice of wife. Only once have I heard a woman reject her son's or brother's request to help him choose. That was Umm Ali saying to her brother, Ahmed: 'It's you who are to sleep in her arms.'

It is possible for two young people to get married in spite of considerable opposition from the bridegroom's mother. But the bride's mother's approval is seen as an absolute condition for the success of the marriage. This is because she can both manipulate the bride's guardian to refuse a groom she dislikes and, even more, that she strongly guides and influences her daughter's behaviour in the marriage. As one woman put it when I asked why not one of her six brothers and sisters had married a relative on the father's side: 'Because Mummy couldn't stand them!'

Both ideals and realities testify that the mother is the only one who consistently acts in her daughter's own interests, both by formulating them and standing for them. Therefore the mother's presence is seen as essential for preparing a young woman for marriage in the best possible way, both as regards the husband and the dowry. A father is expected to give his daughter in marriage to the first suitor to appear and send her off with an insufficient dowry, partly because he does not know much about the importance of furniture. Thus, for example, a woman was sent into marriage not only with a very small dowry, but moreover without a 'list' (see p. 113) because her father, when relatives encouraged him to write a list, was so naïve that he replied: 'I'm securing the man, not the money.' (*Bashtiri irrägil, mish ilfulús.*) The dowry is seen as the direct product of the mother's efforts and care. On the whole, the role played by her during the whole process of establishing a marriage is a confirmation of the solidarity between mother and child as the only fundamental one in this community.

Conclusion

The expression of some essential features of social life are seen in the conventions surrounding courtship and marriage, and in the specific cases that have been analysed above. Here, as in most societies, the arranging of a marriage serves as a central occasion to activate social relations and express basic values. But in this situation of poverty, it is mainly the interference and the inhibiting effect of other people that are noticeable, and values and folk generalizations about jealousy and mistrust that are expressed.

First, a negative finding: the account I have given above shows that large kin groups do *not* emerge in any of the above situations (i) There is no symbolic expression of their unity as a group in any phase of the rites, nor are they represented by a formal spokesman. This is taken for granted to such an extent that, to take an extreme example, I have seen a bridegroom's father turned away by the bride's mother on his one formal visit to the bride's father before the reading of the Koran, because the bride's father was asleep and should not be disturbed. Elsewhere in the Middle East this would be quite unthinkable. Men there in similar situations act as ambassadors for their families and are treated with the greatest respect, and in certain phases of the rites the whole family group is mobilized and emerges as a unit. (ii) The bride-price and dowry are paid by the bridegroom and the bride's parents without any contribution from other people. This is also different from the practice among Arabs in the Middle East generally, where the bridegroom's family usually contribute to the bride-price. Among poor people in Cairo, however, the bridegroom will often save in a saving club, often in the name of the bride or the bride's mother, with monthly premiums paid in by them. In rare cases his mother may contribute. If the parents are dead, adult brothers will *not* pay their sister's dowry. (iii) The bridegroom acts on his own behalf (partly through spokesmen who may or may not be related). The bride is given away formally by her guardian. If the bride's mother is alive, the agreement must normally meet with her approval, and thus presumably be in harmony with the wishes of the bride. The process is, however, spread out over several stages during a long period, which means the formal parties to the marriage do not have full control of the course of events. Gossip will produce unexpected turns of event and create new situations which influence events. In other words, even if the decisions are made by individuals rather than by large family corporations as happens in most of the Middle East, they are to a large extent decided by a more diffuse network of involved people, spinning intrigues.

Poverty strongly affects these processes. Envy and gossip are general features of Egyptian culture but are intensified in a poor environment. Seeds of doubt regarding the match are planted in both parties, and this increases the risk of complications. The fact that corporations are poorly developed can also be traced back to poverty (see Chapter 5). Negotiations and agreements have a typically unstable character: they are individual promises rather than collective commitments. Poverty also leads to a more general undermining of the concepts of honour and their implications in daily life. The intensification of slander (*xubs*) and gossip (*kalâm innás*), and the dissolution of family corporations lead to a disintegration of public concensus, dividing it into unstable shifting networks and small alliances. No matter how badly a person acts (from a moral point of view) he can always mobilize support for his action among people who are enemies of the object of his action. He is thereby not negatively sanctioned for his actions, but is assured an approving audience in one of several of the fighting factions. In that way a man can sit boasting, with everyone's approval, that he got back the ring from his former fiancée by pretending he wanted to have 'Yours Forever' engraved in it, before breaking the engagement.

Finally, let us consider what foundations are laid down for future married life. Some mothers express their belief that when the young couple get to know each other before the wedding, in the way that we have seen in this chapter, it will make it easier for them to live happily together after the wedding. This is doubtful. The contact which the parties have before the marriage is so restricted by the contexts in which they are allowed to meet that they will commonly

only show their best side in a very restricted sphere of activity. The only side the man reveals in his role as a fiancé is the extent to which he wishes to control the woman's dress and freedom of movement, attitudes which will, of course, be important in the life awaiting her as his wife (engagements are occasionally broken for this particular reason). As for the man, I doubt whether he learns anything essential about his fiancée. The important thing is that all activities which will take place within marriage are of a completely different character, especially where the man is concerned, from anything ever experienced before. From being supported by his parents while earning an income which, on the whole, he can spend on himself (except for extensive saving for the bride-price), the man now acquires the full financial responsibility for household expenses. Both will be forced to make mutual decisions and adapt themselves to extensive mutual demands within the framework of a precarious economy. Moreover, the very relationship between them has already become a fighting issue between persons who continue to be part of their social life, and who will continue to influence them and go on spinning intrigues.

SEVEN
Role formation within marriage

Married women are the central characters in the neighbourhood, and an understanding of their behaviour, values, and goals is essential to an understanding of the neighbourhood as a social system. Because all these women are dependent on their husbands, their behaviour is largely conditioned by the relationship between husband and wife. To analyse how features of this relationship arise, I must make a complex role analysis in which I give a detailed description of the tactics employed by husbands and wives and the constraints under which they operate. In the preceding chapter we saw how spouses start their married life with little knowledge of one another, although their relationship is already troubled: they have been through complicated preliminaries full of distrust, disappointment, and negotiated compromises, in which other persons have been and still are actively involved. The further development of their roles takes place in the context of a poverty which creates a perpetual discrepancy between on the one hand, the ideals and obligations connected with the statuses of wife and husband, and on the other hand the reciprocal services and benefits that can be provided in practice. Before I give the data, however, I shall give a sketch of two women's lives so as to depict the social reality which we are trying to penetrate and understand. I quote directly from my field notes.

Umm Mohammed is a twenty-two-year-old woman, married to Ahmed, thirty-two. They have been married for eight years and have three children.

One evening at about half past ten I come to her flat and find her sitting alone knitting. It's obvious that she is very worried about something. I ask after Ahmed and get an anxious reply. She doesn't know where he is, he did not come home for lunch today as he should. She has no idea where he is or what may have happened. If only he had a steady afternoon job, then she could have enquired there. Now she is quite helpless. I sympathize whole-heartedly and then her confidences come pouring out: all about Ahmed, who in the past two months has strayed on a dangerous path – manipulated by his father's (young) wife. 'I hardly ever see him at home these days. Whenever he is free, he goes to see his father and sits there smoking hashish, playing cards and telling jokes. Sometimes he doesn't even come home for lunch but goes straight to his father. Other days he just stops for food, changes his clothes, and goes directly to his father. Then he comes back again at about nine at night to collect Abdullah (his best friend). They say they're going to see one of Abdullah's friends. Sometimes he even says he's going to drive the cab (Ahmed's extra job). I don't believe him, so I wait for a while, and send Mohammed (seven-year-old son) to his granddad to see. Ahmed is always there. One day I came there myself and surprised him at it. He got furious and shouted: "Are you coming to spy on me, you bitch, you daughter of a whore! (*ya wisha, ya bint kálb*) I'm free! I shall divorce you at the end of Ramadan – you whore!"' (Divorce during Ramadan is sinful.)

Also, Ahmed spends a lot of money on clothes and amusements for the father's family. Last Tuesday, for example, he bought material for two *gallabaias* (pyjamas/nightdresses) for each of the six members of the family. Not only that, but Gamila (Umm Mohammed's younger sister) has even seen Ahmed's new shoes which cost him £1.35 on the feet of Fathi (the stepmother's son).

Umm Mohammed is feeling bitter, because this is the month of Ramadan and her family consequently has more need for money than usual. Among other things, the family owes rent for two months, and she has even had to sell her golden earrings to give the children new clothes for the festivities.

'This type of life has been going on now for two whole months. But last night when Ahmed came home at midnight the third night running this week, I exploded: confronted him and tried to make him understand that he is making life impossible for me. He is my husband and so I expect him to come straight home from work, change his clothes, eat in peace and quiet, have a rest and on free nights sit with me and the children or take us out walking or on a visit somewhere. I told him that the house which he leaves he should also return to (*Ilbēt illi xārig mīn mafrud yirgáçlu*) – not go straight to his father's house from work as he often does now.

Ahmed was furious and shouted at me: "I'm a free man! All you have here is the right to your food!" (*Ana ḥurr. Líki takli bass.*)

I replied that I had had the food in my father's house and that I hadn't married him for that. And if he expects me to shut up as long as he lets me have the food, he might as well take his clothes and move in with his father for good. So that I know what I have – a house without a man – and can adjust to that. Then I won't have to be constantly hurt and disappointed the way I am now because I keep hoping and waiting.'

Umm Mohammed explains that she has intentionally started to quarrel with Ahmed at a very early stage to teach him how dangerous his new path is. 'To teach a man is like teaching a child: both have to be reproached and punished at an early stage. Left to their own devices they will follow the wrong path throughout life.'

She compares their present life with their life as an engaged couple:

'At first I didn't care much for Ahmed, I was so young, only thirteen, and I didn't understand a thing. But as I got to know him, I became very fond of him, and he was very fond of me. He would come and see us almost every evening and stay until midnight. He cared for me a lot (*kán biyxâf qawi çaleyya*). If I had only a slight stomach pain, he would rush up and want to take me to the doctor. We went to the cinema together, went walking and went to see his relatives. Look at the difference now! Now he leaves us on our own and doesn't care about a thing. When he comes back late at night and finds me and Umm Hussein (her best friend) sitting there he just rushes past us with only an "Excuse me!" (*an iznuku*), and goes straight to bed. In the morning he is tired and irritable when I try to wake him up, he calls me daughter of a bitch/whore and I only just manage to get him out of bed. Then he has a glass of tea with milk – without a word. And goes off.

And that's how it usually goes. As time passes a wife becomes cheaper to her husband (*hiyya bitibqa açla çalèh*).

But Ahmed still loves me. That's not the problem. All the troubles are due only to his stepmother's manipulation.'

I have related this story in full detail to show the emotional register of attitudes and expections of a married woman in this poor quarter. That this was not a unique, isolated case, may be seen from another woman's summary of her marriage. The woman is

Umm Ali, thirty-three years old, married to Hassan, forty-three. They have six children aged from two to eighteen.

'I was only fifteen when we got married, and I saw marriage as something terrifying because I was so young. Hassan used to come over to see my sister's husband – they were friends – that was how he saw me. At first he asked to marry Karima [older sister] but she refused because he is black. [Hassan is half Sudanese.] But I thought he was handsome and followed Mum's advice to marry him.

While we were engaged, Hassan used to take me out with my sister. We went to the cinema, to cafés and the Zoo. But this happy time ended abruptly when the marriage was consummated. Hassan spent all his time in bad company, he smoked hash and drank whisky with them. I did know that Hassan had these habits before we got married, but I had thought that all would be well once we had our own home and he could get away from the bad influence of his friends. Instead the opposite happened: Hassan ignored me completely. He came and went as it suited him, and beat me and abused me when I asked him where he had been or tried to teach him about the dangers of the path he had chosen. It was on such occasions that I lost my front teeth. But it was my brother-in-law's fault that Hassan behaved like this.[1] For he encouraged him to beat me and not accept any interference: to play the role of the strong man!

I was left on my own all day long with my sad thoughts. I wept as I walked back and forth, back and forth in the flat. Late at night when Hassan came home life became even more unbearable, for he beat me and shouted at me and seemed to torment me intentionally – to *dominate* me. For example he would ask me to serve the food, then take it out, bring it in, take it out, etc. ... Afterwards when we were in bed he wanted to make love to me. While I was crying ... Couldn't he understand that this kind of life was impossible? At first shouting and beating and ignoring and then "completely together" (*sawa sawa*) in bed. How *could* he expect me to make love to him?

I was so desperate because I had expected marriage to be *sharing*, doing things *together*, we two; that Hassan would come home from work and then we would be together at home and when he was free we would go out walking together in the park.

---

[1] The traditional scapegoats, the mother-in-law and sister-in-law were not possible to use in this case, because Hassan's mother was dead and his sister lived in Sudan.

In the beginning I made myself beautiful for him, I put on rouge and mascara and was so pretty when he came home. But then I saw that it did not have any effect, and ever since I have neglected my looks...

I tried to make Hassan understand that we had to be open with each other and mutually adjust, on both sides: that we had to tell what each one of us expected and wished from life, so that we could make each other happy. But he was disdainful and only replied: "I do as it suits me!" (*Báçmil illi mazági!*) or "I'm free" (*ana ḥurr*).

I had wanted to teach Hassan about life so that he could distinguish good from evil, something he never learnt because he lost his mother as a baby. But he kept obstinately to his old ways, so he wore himself out, and us as well (*Tíçib wa tiçibna gambu*). If a marriage is to succeed the two must stand together (*lázim ilitnēn qalbuhum maça baçd* – literally: it is necessary that the hearts of the two be together). Just like two people who start a business together: it is doomed to fail unless they cooperate.'

These two women express a view common among the women in the poor quarter about what the wife desires most from her husband, and how she experiences her own actual situation.

To the woman the marriage is a most fundamental and central relation – only by and through it can she hope to achieve what she prizes most highly in life: a shared life with a man who gives her love and care and who needs her. She can be a mother and be addressed as *Umm* – and be a housewife (*'sitt ilbēt'*) i.e. have the right to her own flat. So precious is the husband in his capacity as her only source of these values that almost regardless of what he does she cannot afford to interpret his action as a sign of lack of tenderness or love for her, but chooses to look for scapegoats. The man's unique importance to the woman can be summarized by the following straightforward statement of one woman: '[to have] a husband who makes sure that she and the children have what they need in the way of food and clothes, looks after her, sits at home with her when he is free or takes her and the children out for a walk – that's all in the world to a woman (*da kulli she'li ma'ra*). But only one out of a hundred lives up to it,' she adds resignedly.

Why does the man not want to join the woman in such a close relationship, but chooses to insist on his independence and autonomy? When there is such a lack of complementarity in the values they pursue in marriage, it is natural to look for an explanation in

Role formation within marriage 101

the alternatives available to the wife and the husband in their situation, as each sees it.

First, let us look at the husband's situation, and focus upon the home which is the scene for nearly all his interaction with his wife. Because he is the only provider, and because he has a right to command the work of his wife, his is the final responsibility for how the home appears. No matter how hard he works, it will stand, with all its blemishes and shortcomings, as a monument to his failures. He is so ashamed of it that he does not want his friends to see it. (See chapter 4.) There is a lot of noise from children who use each other mainly as toys. (Even one of the two 'good' fathers in the material (see p. 71) explains that he has to stay away from home in his free time, or he will easily come to beat his children.) He is met by a wife whose appearance is another proof of his failure and who emphasizes it for him even more by her constant nagging about money. The lack of money hits him also in other painful ways: he will come home tired and hungry, there is no food waiting and he is told it's his own fault because he brought the money too late; or he comes home hungry *and* with money for food, but the wife refuses to go out to buy food for him because it is dark outside; or he does not like the food that is served, and rushes up, shouting: 'Do you call this *food?*', to be met with 'Do you call this *money?*' He finds out that she has borrowed money although he has forbidden her over and over again to do so. The children are ill and need medical attention, he does not have the money. They need clothes and school books and a thousand other things which he cannot get them. On ritual occasions in the family, such as the circumsision of a son or daughter, everyone expects him to bring home a present, and they reproach him when he does not.

In such a situation, what can the man hope to realize of himself? It seems obvious that it is so little that he will try to find alternatives, if there are any. To what other arenas, then, does the man have access, and what can he achieve there?

The man is mobile. Unlike the woman, he can come and go as he likes. Poverty drives him to spend most of his time working (see p. 29). In the little spare time he has, he wants to relax. This he can do by seeking the company of friends in cafés where, conforming to fundamental values, he is together with men in a place which will not compromise him. The café certainly calls for money, but in relatively small amounts. Alternatively, he can go to see his female relatives. They will *always* be ready to give him support and recognition, explain away his failures and praise his efforts, and the interaction takes place in a home for which he does not bear the responsibility. Judging by the material I collected it is obvious that the man also wants tenderness and emotional support from his wife. Marriages entered into because of love and against the wishes of the family i.e. mother and sisters (such as Abdullah's, p. 114) are expressions of such values. It is also striking how often men emphasize their ability to show tenderness and love as personal qualities. The same emphasis is also implicit in another example, a conversation where I said I couldn't keep a dog in a town flat because it needs fresh air and exercise. Spontaneously the husband exclaimed to his wife: 'You see! They care both for animals and people! Here people say: Don't bother! (*Hyalla*).'

When the husband nonetheless chooses a strategy towards his wife which does not aim at realizing tenderness or intimacy as values, the reasons for this are obvious. Emotional involvement with the woman and her world, the activities in the home, would imply a deeper involvement with his own failure. After a long, exhausting working day which, by any standard, has brought little reward, he wants relaxation, peace, *detachment* from all which is his economic responsibility. Accordingly, he wants from his wife and his family a relationship which assures the following for him: a clean and tidy house, the food cooked, the bed made, the children well behaved, and the wife ready for work or sex when he wants it. In other words, he does *not* want a self-realizing relationship, but a practical and economical service: a wife who is happy and satisfied with whatever *he* can give her! This implies loyalty, and the expectation that she will not compromise him by borrowing money from others. To the man, I think that these are the most powerful expressions of love a woman can give. They communicate submission, recognition, and respect.

The man will be supported by other women, primarily his female relatives, in his view that these expectations are reasonable. They will *always* be prepared to point out and condemn how his wife does violence to the ideals: i.e. to make do with the money he gives her (see p. 57) be economical, keep the house tidy, look after his clothes, not limit his freedom, etc. It even happens that women resignedly hold up such ideals to themselves, as can be seen from this quotation: 'I don't complain and don't make scenes when my husband says he has no money. I don't answer contemptuously, "Why not?" like most women and leave the house. I adjust to the weather.' (*mashya māça iggaww.*)

What the husband wants from marriage is a relationship which conforms to his conventional rights. He will certainly not sit at home or go for a walk with the family in his spare time. On the

Role formation within marriage 103

contrary, he wants to be a strong man among other men, autonomous and independent. The best solution for him is therefore to insist on his own conventional rights (which he knows will be supported in a possible mediation), and to defend these rights with the sanctions he has by virtue of his status. Among other things, he holds the trump card in his hand: the sole right to dissolve the marriage, thereby also separating the mother from her children.

His status as a husband, however, also entails obligations. As we have seen repeatedly, he does not fulfil these very well. In his relationship to his wife he can therefore hardly make use of the sanctions which are normally applicable in a relationship of reciprocity: to hold back his contributions. The woman already has so many outstanding demands on him that she sees herself as *sāḥib ilḥaqq* – 'the owner of the right'.

If he deprives her of further value, she will answer tit for tat: fulfilling *her* obligations (even) less. These conditions tempt the man to exaggerated use of the ultimate sanctions of the husband status: *authority dramatization* and *threats of divorce*. We have already seen an example of the first in Umm Ali's story about Hassan, who commands her to take the food to and from the table. Variations on the same theme are to command work from the wife when she is ill or tired, e.g. tell her to sweep the floor where he is going to sit when he eats, or to insist after a quarrel on her performing acts which are particularly clear symbols of submission, such as tying his shoelaces.

Threats of divorce are extremely frequent and are often made during quarrels that arise over trifles. We have already seen examples of this in the episode of the man who came home when his wife helped the neighbour who was giving birth (see p. 55) and also in Umm Mohammed's story. A whole register of abuse – whore! daughter of a bitch/whore! slut! – accompany and precede the threat. An illustration of a short, typical course of events of this kind is the following. Two children were playing, and happened to break the glass over a picture of their paternal grandfather. The father was furious with the mother: 'Get out! You daughter of a whore! I'm divorcing you! Go and get my sister so that she can look after me! You can't bring up my children ... Go away to your father!'

Given this role solution for the man, how can the woman counter it? How can she *defend* her rights, *improve* her ability to use counter-sanctions and *shape a role solution* that gives her a maximum of the values she is seeking to realize in life as a whole?

The woman seems to seek six main forms of value: material

goods, love, recognition, social status, children, and house. Some important aspects of these forms of value will be found in *Table 7(1)* below, showing from whom she gets them and to whom she gives them.

It should be clear how unique her relationship with her husband is. He is the single or the primary source of most of these highly esteemed values. But some other values, such as friendship, she cannot realize at all through him, and for some of the values, she has alternative sources.

Because the husband's female relatives compete with her for his money and affection, the wife has to develop a strategy aiming at two targets simultaneously: to defend and strengthen her position towards her husband, and to prevent others from using him as their source. Since she, unlike her husband, lacks categorical sanctions, her most important means are the following:

(1) *Demands* for material values which she legitimizes by the rights she has by virtue of her status, such as urging her husband to satisfy hers and the children's needs before giving anything at all to his relatives. She knows this view will be supported in principle in a possible mediation. She supports her demands with sanctions based on the reciprocal character of social relations: fulfilling her obligations with less care and greater reluctance, as regards both services and loyalty. Moreover, she can make life unpleasant for her husband by provoking a situation where she is not on speaking terms with him, forcing him to humble himself and take the initiative for each non-programmed service he wants from her.

(2) *The children*, whom she now uses against her husband (see Chapter 5), both by forming their character and thus their whole attitude to their father, and by mobilizing support, possibly intervention, from older children for herself in a possible confrontation. The degree of effectiveness the woman achieves in this game can be illustrated by the fact that all the adult men I know normally avoid any contact with their fathers.

(3) *Male relatives*, who take on the part of mediators. They are obliged to defend her interests against her husband and, being men, can negotiate with him as partners on an equal footing within a system of mutual understanding. Thereby they can manoeuvre not only by appealing to the rights her status entails but also to folk wisdom (e.g. that mother-in-law and daughter-in-law *must* live separately).

(4) *Resort to relatives* (male or female) who will shelter her until the husband personally collects her, and in front of witnesses makes the necessary concessions. If the husband does not have the

facility of a grown-up daughter or a female relative to do the housework, his wife by this strategy will place him in an acutely difficult situation, and usually after two to three days he will take the initiative for a reconciliation.

(5) *The forming of alliances* with one or more of the man's relatives against a mutual enemy, usually another relative (see p. 111).

But how can these sanctions be effective? In comparison to the man's sanctions they seem quite secondary.

Table 7(1): *Scheme of forms of values sought by women*

form of value	received from
material goods:	
money	husband (maintenance), possibly brother/other male relatives on the father's side
food	husband, mother, sister, intimate woman-friend (reciprocal)
clothes	husband, relatives – after demands from the woman (reciprocal)
ritual gifts	close woman-friend (reciprocal) brother, father
moral support/ recognition:	husband, family of marriage, well-disposed blood relatives, women-friends, allies (all these reciprocal)
love/attention	husband, mother, brother, sister/woman -friend (all these reciprocal)
refuge	mother, father, sister, blood relative on mother's side (reciprocal), brother (reciprocal)
status	neighbours (reciprocal)
children	husband

The tactical situation between the spouses is one in which the husband has already been driven to the ultimate sanction, threat of divorce, over trifles. However, for him to put this threat into effect would entail great expense on his part. He would have to pay alimony to his wife (*náfçit issana*) of ¼ of his wages for a whole year. (To receive the money the woman probably has to go through a court, which demands expertise, time, and about £50 to pay counsel.) Then he will have to pay her *muaxxar issudaq* – the outstanding part of the bride-price (see p. 82) – in a lump sum. The size of the amount seems to vary between £10 and £50. If his wife has a *qaima* – a list of her material belongings – (see p. 84) as most women do, she takes all the furniture in the flat, including cooking vessels and bedclothes, with her when she goes. If the man does not have access to the services of a mother, daughter, or sister, he will soon have to get himself a new wife, which will cost him both money and trouble. Even if he takes a wife who is not a virgin, he will have to pay a bride-price, possibly even buy her furniture and utensils himself. This is very expensive in relation to his wages (see Chapter 3 and the Appendix for prices). If he has children and they are under seven or nine, he has to pay alimony for them until they can move into his house. If the children are older, he will be confronted with new problems by way of the stepmother/stepchildren syndrome.

These costs make divorce a solution for the man only in cases where conditions in the marriage are extremely unsatisfactory. Once the threat of divorce has been made, it becomes a frightening reality to both parties. Mediators must be brought in to reconcile the spouses and they will formulate demands and counter-demands which both parties will have to accept. To the man it is a question of playing it in such a way that he secures his rights while seeming to give in under pressure. When he takes his wife back, this is also an implicit acknowledgement of her value to him. What is more he risks having his wife scorning him for not *daring* to carry out the threat. In that case he gives her another trump card to play.

Because the man is so reluctant to carry out the threat of divorce, it is important for him to find less drastic sanctions. He needs tactics whereby he can make daily life difficult and painful for his wife if he so wishes, without resorting to the ultimate threats. Briefly, he must pay her back in her own coin.

The man can resort to several standardized techniques. He can hurt her and create doubts in her about his love by a series of measures: emphasizing the beauty and good character of other women; giving her the impression that he is not jealous by, for example, encouraging her to go to distant places on her own; saying things like: 'You are ready for retirement!' when she is twenty years old; ignoring her completely when he is at home; sharing none of his daily experiences with her; never praising her; etc. (Thus a man complained about his employer who never praised him, and in the next breath defended his use of the same tactics against his wife: 'or else she will believe she's indispensable and put on airs and graces.') Demonstratively seeking the company of his female relatives, her main rivals and arch enemies, is the husband's most effective way of making his wife jealous and insecure about both his money and his love. Another good strategy is to criticize her by praising others. Since his authority over her is total, he can also rob her of value on the larger stage where she appears: he can in fact lock her up in the house, refuse her any contact with friends and even her mother or other female relatives — a very painful punishment for any woman. When the interaction becomes too problematical for him, he can, like her, break it off by provoking a condition where they are not on speaking terms. One man would do this regularly during Ramadan for eight years to avoid demands for new clothes. It was not until I provided the family with new clothes that they celebrated Ramadan together.

The man's status is based on the fact that he is the head of the family both in the legal and the economic context. However, the extent of his power depends upon which of these secondary sanctions he chooses to apply in combination with his conventional and legal sanctions, dramatization of authority and threat of divorce. The woman's power on the other hand, is determined by which of the five measures she controls, and naturally, by how much personal strength and confidence she manages to show. The relative influence of the spouses on each other and on their own situation is determined by the balance between their respective sources of power, and this will affect their actual moves and counter-moves, i.e. their role solutions.

This argument does not imply that the spouses are involved in constant political manoevring vis-à-vis each other. They can also participate in a happy, relaxed atmosphere, where the husband plays with the children — there is fun and laughter and a flow of mutual give and take. Marriages differ of course, but in most people's lives I think the confrontations are rarer than quiet routine life. My point is, however, that in the course of most marriages so many outstanding demands are accumulated by both parties, there is so much latent material for conflicts, that any spark will produce a large explosion. When this is the case, it is probable that the explosions are much less dramatic to the people themselves than to the anthropologist. What is certain is that such dramatic confrontations occur with *great* frequency and that the relationship with the spouse is, at least for the woman, continuously problematic.

The woman's role solutions at different stages of life

Most conflicts between husband and wife can be subsumed under three headings: *money, the wife's female relatives, the husband's female relatives.* Throughout life these are the primary sources of difficulties between them. The shape of the difficulties which ensue will change over time, and this reflects changes of both husband's and wife's positions over the years.

I will therefore portray the woman's role solutions at three stages of marriage: (1) as newly married, (2) with small children, (3) with teenage children.

(1) The newly married woman

Adjustment to marital status is a difficult and slow process for both parties. The poor themselves maintain that the husband will often resort to extreme dramatization of authority during the first months, including physical violence (see Hassan p. 99), while the woman frequently, and sometimes for long periods, escapes back to her mother. The folk theory is that the husband's behaviour is due to the financial responsibility he has suddenly acquired. The probability of divorce seems to be greater at this stage than at any later time. Five men and two women in the material have such a background. Egyptian national statistics show a similar clear tendency: about 50 per cent of all divorces take place between spouses who have been married for less than two years. Each of the spouses has strong ties to his or her relatives, and little or no mutual trust and solidarity have been established. The parties' relatives on each side, above all mother and older sister, have a one-sided loyalty to their own and protect their pre-established interest in this person by striving to place him or her in the best possible starting position vis-à-vis the spouse. Such help seems primarily to take the form of guidance in the art of manoeuvring and manipulation, for which newly married, inexperienced couples feel a great need. After the frequent conflicts between them both are expected to seek the support of their families. According to people this commonly involves lying about the spouse, which contributes to further antagonizing the spouse and the in-laws. People emphasize how important it is therefore for married couples to avoid their in-laws after such conflicts: the in-laws will be eager to seize the opportunity of hurling accusations at the new son-in-law or daughter-in-law.

The man's resolution of extreme dramatization of authority seems to be meant as a move against anticipated manipulation. No doubt the man has numerous experiences, from his own home as well as those of others, of women manipulating men. Certainly he knows the folk generalizations saying that they do, and if he has female relatives they will warn him in no uncertain terms. The woman on her side learns that a man must be tackled with all the devices of the art of manipulation, and be *brought up* as quickly as possible to the behaviour she wishes. Among other things, she must secure the maximum flow of money from him by demanding from the very start '*hāt – hāt!*' – give me, give me!

The following story may serve as an example of extreme interference by the in-laws. A man came to his mother-in-law's house to collect his wife after a visit. He carried a covered basket of food given to him by his mother, and was impatient to go home straight away. The next day, when he was out working, his mother-in-law, furious, came to the wife and commanded her to 'escape' back home, because that lout of a husband of hers had not given *her* any of the food! The daughter did not dare to do anything but obey.

Under threat of such intervention from his wife's female relatives, the best strategy for the man is to refuse to let her see them. The prohibition can however be adhered to only if he himself has the courage to refuse them contact, since the wife could never bring herself to do it. One mother was furious because her newly married daughter had refused to wash her clothes, on the instructions of her husband. This was his counter-move after she had given refuge to the daughter for forty days and forbidden her to go with him when he came to collect her, but her indignation turned against the daughter as the clothes-washing issue developed. An older man in the sample has not been on speaking terms with his mother-in-law, who lives ten metres down the street, since he was newly married twenty-two years ago! The reason he gave was that she kept asking his wife to do things for her all the time, like washing and cooking.

The problems which the woman's in-laws will create for her are best solved by her avoiding contact with them as much as possible. Amongst other things, the first confrontation between them will establish a condition of not being on speaking terms, which means the mother-in-law and the older sister-in-law cannot reach her with demands for work. Everyone knows that in-law relations between women are fraught with conflicts and it is therefore in the husband's own interest to keep the parties separated. Six of the women in the sample began their married life in a flat with their mother-in-law and/or sister-in-law. But life soon became unbearable, and most had to move after only a couple of months.

Folk wisdom about the threat posed by both husband's and wife's families through their conflicting interests and constant interference sometimes make a newly married couple decide to settle down far away from both families to give themselves the best possible start to their marriage.

(2) The woman with small children

How do five to ten years of marriage affect the relationship between husband and wife? The spouses have come to know each other better and are more able to judge and predict each other's reactions. Children have been born. According to some men, this makes women conceited. What is quite certain is that children give women increased personal security and strength, and that the parents are united in a new mutual interest. Men often seem genuinely fond and proud of their small children. A little episode may serve as an example. A father devoted himself to playing with the smallest child of six months, and seemed quite jealous whenever she showed any interest in anyone else, including the mother. Only a few months before, however, he had been beside himself with despair over yet another mouth to feed. During play, he suddenly exclaimed: 'What a pity that these lovely little ones become so big and cumbersome!'

The themes of conflict are still strong but are probably more routine and have more standardized solutions: the husband and wife have learnt to estimate how far they can go on the basis of the experience of the relative costs of different tactics. The eternally present problem, money, is solved by the woman by unswerving demands for her recognized rights and dramatization of the children's needs (see p. 69). Apart from this, she will borrow money whenever she needs to, in spite of the costs this entails, such as fits of fury and perhaps threats of divorce from the husband.

In-law relations most of the time are now seen as less threatening because the woman has become stronger and the husband more committed to and dependent on his new family. I have seen several cases where the husband at this stage of life has taken an unequivocal stand for his new family against his own relatives, both in the competition between them for his moral support and affection, and for his money. He can maintain, for example, in agreement with the folk theory and his wife's wishes, that he has to provide for the children Allah has given *him*, before taking any responsibility for others, be they the children of his father, brother, or sister. The material also suggests that the husband is less prepared than before to give unconditional moral support to his family of birth. The explanation of this is perhaps that he is less dependent on them because he has learnt techniques to handle his wife himself. Therefore he dares react more strongly when they fail in *their* obligations to him.

Refuge with relatives and appeal to male defenders continue to

Role formation within marriage   111

be important tactics for the woman. She also seeks to form alliances with people who are important to the husband, in order to increase the pressure on him. One of the most elegant pieces of manipulation that I have ever seen can serve as an illustration to this method: the individuals involved here are the same as in the case described in pp. 96-100.

One afternoon, after playing with the children, Ahmed wanted to put on his shoes to go and see his father and stepmother. Umm Mohammed reacted quickly but jocularly by grabbing one of his shoes, trying to take it away from him, saying: 'No, tonight you shall sit here with us, you went to see them this morning!' (Ahmed had been ill for a couple of days.) 'Are we not humans too − are we animals?' As they tugged at each end of the shoe, and Ahmed tried to push her away, Umm Mohammed continued: 'OK, if you want to, go then, but why don't you bring me along?' 'Because you can't make conversation!' he replied. Then Umm Mohammed started to persuade him to come with her instead to his sister Umm Ali to watch television: 'Let's go to her (pointing at her baby daughter Mirvat) aunt − she *loves* Mirvat!' By exploiting the fact that he would make his sister so happy by taking the daughter to see her she eventually made him give in − with the attitude of a father who lets a child have her way. Umm Mohammed was radiant and triumphant when they set out. As an observer of the episode I was very impressed by her tactics. It's obvious that she could never have achieved the same result by nagging and attacking her husband. That he would have seen as interference with his liberty. The next day when I congratulated her on her performance, she told me that it was her sister-in-law, Umm Ali, who had given her the recipe! Thus two women chose to play down strong conflicting interests between themselves to score against a mutual enemy. (Umm Ali's and Ahmed's stepmother.) Alliances of this type are very frequent.

The problems which the woman's family may create and the solutions that result may be illustrated with one example. This is directly connected with the story at the beginning of this chapter, and took place the following day. I went to see Ahmed's and Umm Mohammed's best friends and nearest neighbours, the married couple Abdullah and Umm Hussein. They told me that Ahmed and Umm Mohammed had had a violent quarrel after I had gone (it is easy to overhear quarrels from flats nearby) and that he had again threatened her with divorce as soon as Ramadan was over. Both expressed deep sympathy with Ahmed, for his problem was Umm Mohammed's family, the mother and two teenage sisters, who were always in his flat. No wonder he escaped to his father's house! They criticized Umm Mohammed harshly for saying: 'I love my mother more than my husband, for she bore me and brought me up.' This attitude they found quite wrong. But at the same time they emphasized that Umm Mohammed's dilemma was real. For even if she wished to obey her husband and keep the relatives at bay, how could it be done? 'What can she do? Talk like that to her mother? Unthinkable!' (*Hiyya hatiçmil eh? Hatitkallim ummaha? Mish maqúl!!*)

From Umm Hussein I went to Umm Ali who was also eager to tell me about Ahmed and Umm Mohammed. Ahmed had come to see her the same day and then she had asked him to spend less time with the father. (Umm Mohammed had been to see her and urged her to help.) Ahmed had replied that it was none of her business. He is his own master. And Umm Ali defended Ahmed:

> 'Umm Mohammed is unfair to him because she never lets him have any peace and quiet or a chance to rest. Her family are *always* there. Once Ahmed came to me and tore up his shirt in despair. "*Ha'ísh izzay!*" "How can I live in this way?" Sometimes he explodes in front of them, and then they'll stay away for a couple of days. But then they start coming again, just as often Umm Mohammed does not know the art of looking after her husband. Her first duty is to him, the mother must come second. She should make sure he has everything he needs and finds his home peaceful and tidy when he comes home. And then she must leave him to spend his free time as he likes, to the greatest possible extent, not complain when he wants to go here or there, as Umm Mohammed does when Ahmed says he wants to go and see one of his sisters! She irritates him with her constant: "Is there no taxi free today?" [Ahmed works extra as a cab driver. The demand for cars which are hired from the owners is greater than the supply.] When a woman nags her husband she only makes him obstinate.'

These comments give rise to several questions. When life is made unbearable for Ahmed because of Umm Mohammed's relatives, and she cannot tell them to go away, why can *he* not do something to keep them away? As a husband he has total authority over his wife!

The answer may be that he is afraid of Umm Mohammed's counter-moves in case he deprives her of the value she attaches to the company of, and the fulfilment of duties to her mother. She could pack up her things and move to her mother's for good. He himself does not have the alternative of sanctioning her by moving temporarily to his father's, as Umm Mohammed in the opening story encouraged him to do; the father and stepmother would then probably try to drain him of further material resources, and his financial situation is difficult enough as it is. Moreover, their flat is extra-overcrowded because the stepmother's daughter has already taken refuge there with three children. Another case where the husband *has* managed to rid himself of the presence of his mother-in-law when *he* is at home may serve as a test of this explanation: the man in question is just as badly off as Ahmed, has no relatives to escape to, but neither has his wife. She has moreover a father divorced from her mother, to whom he has been able to appeal. But even with such strong measures he has not achieved what he really wanted: to forbid the mother-in-law any access to his flat, something he intensely wants to do because he is sure she eats their food.

In other words, the woman's family remains a real problem to the man, whereas his is not to the same extent a problem to the woman. This becomes specially obvious and acute because it is the *woman* who rules in the house. Consequently, his family stay away and hers come.

To take refuge with male relatives, and to use them as defenders are particularly important sanctions for the woman. Their importance can be seen most clearly in one case where the main actor lacks recourse to either, and is in the most unfavourable position possible with her husband generally. She lives in a flat with her in-laws and brother-in-law (which in itself is an implication of her lack of assets), and moreover, she does not have a 'list' of her belongings (*qaima*). The woman is the above-mentioned Umm Hussein, and the following episode shows the pervasive influence of her in-laws on her life.

These events took place on the second day of Ramadan. At sunset the main meal of the day is eaten as one of the great family feasts of the year. Umm Hussein's husband Abdullah was away at work, and she was sitting crying from loneliness whilst preparing the food for herself and the children. Her in-laws and their children were eating in a bakery they run not far away. Ahmed and Umm Mohammed, who live in the flat adjoining hers, felt very sorry for her and invited her to eat with them. During the meal Umm Hussein's brother-in-law came home and saw them because they had left the door to the entrance hall open. He immediately reported the event to his mother and sister (*not* to his father) and they were furious. They didn't say one word to Umm Hussein when they came home that evening, just looked at her contemptuously. But when Abdullah came home late at night, they descended on him: 'She is impolite and shameless and her father hasn't brought her up properly!' (As mentioned before Umm Hussein's mother died when she was a baby.) Umm Hussein who had been standing listening outside her mother-in-law's room, tore open the door, screaming: 'I'm not at all rude and you shut up about my father!' The in-laws countered with charges that she had eaten with 'a nobody from the street, (i.e. Ahmed) – for he is neither your brother or your father's son!' In rage they then hurled accusations at each other:

'You are of a filthy family (*ya ahla wisxa*) who dare refuse to wash your parents-in-law's working clothes (from the bakery)!'

'I won't wash your filthy clothes!'

'So in the name of Allah your father's dirty laundry must be as clean as snow!' (*Bismillah 'asîl abúki zavy ilfull.*)

Umm Hussein replied by accusing them of not fulfilling *their* obligations to *her*, for example, by giving her miserable third-rate furniture when she was a bride! (Since Umm Hussein only had a stepmother, it was impossible for her to get a dowry from home. Therefore Abdullah saved for furniture for two years before the marriage. He kept the money with his mother, and Umm Hussein is sure that the mother-in-law, who was against the marriage all the time, spent only a fraction of the sum on furniture and took most of the money herself.) This made Abdullah so furious that he beat her across the face with his belt, screaming: 'You shut up!' He had practically never hit her before, and Umm Hussein rushed in to Ahmed and Umm Mohammed. Then Ahmed and Abdullah had to make it up because Abdullah had stood back and let his mother call his best friend 'a nobody from the street'. Abdullah apologized. The following day, Umm Hussein wrote to her father in Alexandria and asked him to come and help her. She and Abdullah were not on speaking terms. (The fact that she was not more severely punished was probably due to Ahmed's intervention with Abdullah.) For the evening meal he invited his parents in and she then lost all appetite and sat down in a corner while the others sat round the table. She received no reply from her father – and she expected none. 'For his wife manipulates him. As you see I have no one in this world except Abdullah.' After not being on speaking terms for ten days Umm Hussein couldn't stand it any longer and took the initiative for a reconciliation. After that Abdullah's parents refused when he invited them. But Umm Hussein was happy not be on speaking terms with them. 'Now they can't reach me with abuses and demands for work.'

From the previous stories we can see how greatly women's

Role formation within marriage 115

positions differ, especially in this phase of life. These differences are partly due to the presence or absence of sources of support, such as places of refuge and male relatives, and partly to skills and strategies that the woman has developed during the marriage. But their effectiveness depends to a large extent on the husband's own position, as illustrated by Ahmed and Abdullah respectively.

(3) The woman with teenage children

After fifteen to twenty years of marriage the husband seems to have become very dependent on his wife and home, and women at this stage of marriage seem very domineering and aggressive. The lack of money, however, still creates constant and grave conflicts. The husband becomes as furious as before when the wife borrows, and the woman's demands have become even more uncompromising. Also, the children have grown up and can themselves make demands on the father.

The principal features of the woman's situation at this stage of life are most clearly revealed in an acute conflict which I observed. This is a family we have already come across, in the story about Gamal's sweater. The further course of the conflict saw Umm Gamal leaving her husband and taking refuge with her father. The husband, Amin, asked me to come with him to mediate. The further course of development is quoted from my field notes:

Amin gets up resolutely, and changes from pyjamas to suit to go over and collect her. On the way he complains bitterly about Umm Gamal's inability to bring up his children, because she is so weak, submissive, and unfair. We arrive at the home of Umm Gamal's father, Ismael. We go in and find Ismael, his wife, their son Mustafa, Mustafa's wife, Umm Gamal, her sister and daughter Mona, all seated. Amin shakes the hand of everyone except his wife. He also avoids looking at her. She on her side stares at him in fury and contempt.

Amin starts by saying that he is there in connection with the quarrel, to sort things out and bring about a reconciliation. Umm Gamal's father Ismael, immediately attacks him: 'You know she is angry because you go out at night!' (The daughter Mona has reported that the father didn't come home until 6.00 a.m. the previous night.)

Amin: 'Out at night! You know that all my life I have been going to *suhur* during Ramadan [last meal before the sunrise at four o'clock] because I can't sleep until then. I have done that all my life.

What right does she have to complain as long as I manage to get up and get to work on time and give her her housekeeping money at the end of the month?'

Ismael is quiet: 'Well...' Then Umm Gamal seizes the initiative, attacking him: 'But you are so greedy, you only think of yourself and of what you can put in your own pocket. You even let your own sons draw knives against each other because of two rotten quid.'

Amin answers back, furiously: 'It wasn't the two quid that the quarrel was all about, it was a matter of principle – we can't be unfair to our children, and spoil them, and waste money at random just as we like, and borrow here and there so that we are constantly in debt.'

Umm Gamal: 'But what else can I do? You don't think of your children! Your children are worse dressed than those whose fathers are in prison!' Her eyes are shining with hatred as she hurls accusations at him: 'The shoes Gamal walks around in are only rags. And he *must* have a sweater to defend and raise his status in front of his friends. Hamdi is selfish not to let him have it, he used to be so nice and now he turns out to be a pansy!' (Common insult.)

Amin interrupts her: 'But don't you understand that we *have to* make do with the £35 which I make a month – it's more than a pound a day! And this month I gave you £55 which you have already wasted because you keep buying things without thinking of what's necessary and unnecessary! Is there any other wife who gets more than one pound a day and complains?' (This argument has a strong effect on all those present – on the women due to envy, and on the men because none of them are able to give anywhere near as much to their wives and are constantly attacked for it.) 'You *eat* up my money – that's what you do! Without a thought for me who must struggle to make it! Out of my bonus of £24 from work this month I took only £4 for myself. Can you call that being selfish?'

She answers angrily (well aware of the strength of his arguments): 'But your children are worse dressed than if their father were dead ... while you – you go out and waste your money, you don't care about them at all!... Yesterday when I went to the cemetery you didn't stay with them at night. No, you left them and stayed out until six in the morning... You went out *gambling* with the money that could have bought Gamal a sweater!'

Her face radiates contempt: 'And all the times over the years that you slept out all night and wasted all your money while we sat at home without food and clothes... while people gossiped about you and even came to us with the gossip... You didn't care at all...'

He interrupts her, screaming accusations, furious: 'You shut up! We are talking about *now*, not the past.' He gets up and goes over to her. 'I want a divorce from you because you attack my present good name and reputation by revealing mistakes from the past which have long been forgotten!'

She gets up, trembling with anger and agitation: 'Yes, you get a divorce from me! Come now, come now, let's go to the *ma'zzun* (the scribe) at once! You find somebody else to bring up your children, I've had enough! I won't set foot in the house of a lout with your character. You divorce me, let's go at once . . . ' She goes towards the door. The whole family follows, grabbing her to stop her: 'Where are you going . . . calm down . . . '

She: 'Let me go! I don't want to see the ugly face of that lout again! I want to go to the *ma'zzun* . . . Didn't he say he wants a divorce? Let him come then! (to Amin) What are you waiting for? Let's get a divorce!'

Amin is standing hesitantly on the threshold.

The family try to hold her back: 'For the sake of your children . . . Where are you to live . . . what will you eat . . . '

She: 'Don't worry! I shan't bother any of *you*! I'm going to my mother's nephew in Masr ilqadima. Let go of me! Leave me alone!'

(It is typical that she would take refuge with a maternal relative.)

The family: 'Come on . . . take it easy . . . just a moment . . . Take it easy, you can go later.' They take her by the arm, her half-brother Mustafa first, and lead her back into the bedroom and push her down into an armchair.

I go into the sitting-room to the men (Amin, Ismael, Mustafa, and an uncle's son who has joined them) to hear Amin's defence speech and see the men's reactions.

Amin is very upset: 'She talks about the past and complains about it, but we are living in the present. Look, how unfair she is to me!' His eyes are begging for understanding. '*You* know how good I am to my wife and family. Every month I give her £35 in housekeeping money, and this month she had £55, and she still complains! Is it not her fault that the £55 wasn't enough? *You* know how much I love my children. Is there any father who is more affectionate than me? But I can't just stand and watch while my wife treats my two sons so differently. One has so many clothes, spends so much pocket money. When his friends come to see him, and I tell him to serve some tea, he isn't satisfied. "Give me money for Pepsi", he says. And I give it to him. The other one has nothing and asks for nothing. He doesn't go out and see his friends, because he only has pyjamas. This year, for the first time ever, he could no longer resign himself to his brother's demands. He asked for something for himself. And what happens? His brother draws a knife against him. Who is to be blamed for such behaviour in my children, such aggression and egotism? Isn't it the mother? Because she gives in one direction when the father is trying to hold back in the other! I have put up with this long enough. But this year I had to call a halt to it and assert my authority in the house, assert my status as a man. In my own house it is I who rule, and there can only be one authority. Since she has proved herself quite incapable of bringing up my children she will have to obey my orders and let me do it!'

Another sister of Umm Gamal, Umm Anwar, has joined the group. Everyone is supporting Amin. Concerning the argument about staying out at night: 'Of course it's your right as a man as long as you go to work properly and give her what you earn. Then she can't say anything about it.'

Amin, happy and relieved, adds that he can't stand sitting inside all night, he feels healthier with some fresh air and exercise. 'And certainly £35 a month is enough!' Umm Anwar: 'All I get is 35p per day! That's £12 a month!' '... and of course she is to blame for the sons's disgraceful behaviour. You are admirable because you try to be fair to your children.'

Umm Anwar takes this opportunity to accuse *her* husband: 'He gives everything to Anwar (eldest son) nothing to Magdi (second eldest). Only this year did Magdi have new clothes because he threatened to complain about his father to the labour protection board.' (Magdi works for his father.) 'Gamal is so selfish...' Amin gets up: 'You know that there is no man who is more affectionate with his children than I am – and with her. You know that I have never ever beaten her...'

The family: 'Yes, we know. She herself brags about how kind you are to her.'

Amin: 'But you know how obstinate she is, if I interfere in her actions, she flies into a rage and does everything to oppose me. I try to make her understand how I want my household to be run. But she won't listen, because she is afraid of the children. For example, now before the festivities, I said: "Don't make any cakes this year – it's so expensive, it's much better we pay off our debt." But the children pressed her, and she gave in and spent a lot of money on 20 kgs of cakes!'

The family: 'Yes, you're right. We know what a responsible and loving husband and father you are. And she is unreasonable. Of course she should stand by you. It's you who have brought her up. Let's see... she lived here for fifteen years... but she's been with you for twenty-five.'

Meanwhile a different scene is taking place in the bedroom: Umm Gamal, her sister, and her half-brother's wife are sitting with her, while her half-brother Mustafa goes in and out between the two rooms. Umm Gamal has been made to sit down in a chair and they are trying to talk sense to her. She shouts at them: 'Go away! I don't want to see you! Don't you worry – I shan't eat in any of your houses or bother you. But I won't set foot in his house again . . .'

The family: 'For the sake of your children . . .'

She: 'Let him get someone else to look after them. You heard what he said – he wants to divorce me . . . Okay, but why isn't he carrying out his threat?' Triumphantly: 'What is he afraid of?'

The family: 'For the sake of Amal!' (The youngest child, five years old, blind and very attached to her mother.) Umm Gamal avoids a direct answer and starts again to blame her husband for all the years when he left them alone without food or clothes . . . The sister: 'But be patient. All those years you sat there patiently, sometimes without anything to eat or drink, while he was out gambling. Now that he's good, why are you so impatient now?'

Mustafa, who is going back and forth between the two rooms, gives her a pat on the cheek: 'Well, well, Feyza (her first name) cool down for our sake. We only want the best for you. Go back home to your children. For where else will you sleep and eat . . . Yes, we know he's done you wrong . . . but forgive him – because we want you here near us. It will soon be all right again, you know . . .' She starts shouting again about being neglected for so many years. The sister: 'For the sake of your children, hold out! For Amal!' She: 'Shut up! I don't want to go home to *his* children. It's *his* fault that the boys are such rascals, for they've had their blood from the father.'

Her uncle's son, a man of the same age as her father, takes her hard by the arm while she struggles against him: 'Come to your senses and go home. The fault is yours, because you brought them up! You are at fault because you're too lax and unfair with your children!'

Amin enters. He goes up to her, kisses her lips, and says: 'Come, I'm in the wrong.' She pushes him away. 'Go away, I'll have nothing to do with you.' He goes.

The uncle's son takes her again by the arm, this time harder and more determinedly: 'It is shameful to act like that. Come now!' She still resists him but is much more submissive and calm this time. Obviously his words have had some impact. She is no longer screaming but says quite calmly: 'No, leave me alone, uncle's son, for I'm unhappy and angry now.' (Implying: 'Yes, I shall go.')

The fact that Amin kissed her made a strong impression on

the female observers. Several times during the following days one could hear them say: 'Look at that! He even kissed her!'

Uncle's son: 'Get up! This is shameful. Didn't you hear him say: "I'm in the wrong"? Then you should go home.'

She is docile now. When the family say: 'For the sake of Unni', and I take her by the arm and ask her to come home just to *see* the children sitting there crying, she gives in. But she emphasizes that she doesn't go home to stay there, only to see the children, and I humour her. On the way home she talks incessantly about his gambling and the long, difficult years. She had become so furious because she had found out that he had been out gambling again the night before the feast. And she told me about the bracelet for £30 which he had given Laila, their daughter, to give her better chances of a good marriage, but then after three weeks he took it away from her again because he needed money himself and Laila is still unmarried, because of her father's bad name and reputation. 'Why else do you think she is sitting there?' And she is furious with her sisters: 'Did you see how they supported him and told me to go home? While I, when they aren't on speaking terms with *their* husbands, I let them come to me and eat my food! That will never happen again!'

Later on that evening, after I leave, the husband and wife are reconciled with the help of Ismael and Uncle's son. The next day Amin gives Gamal the two pounds for the sweater, buys Hamdi a long-sleeved shirt, and collects the dresses for the four daughters from the sewing-woman.

The eternal problem of money can also be seen in another example. Umm Foad had an agreement with her husband that he should give her £12 each month in housekeeping money. One month she only received £10.44 (see p. 39) and immediately rushed to her father in protest. The husband came to collect her and asked her in front of witnesses to agree to lend him the remaining amount of £1.56, to be repayable next month. The wife utterly refused. She did not agree to go home until she got her £12, which was made possible by her father lending his son-in-law the £1.56. This event is typical of the woman's basic attitude to the man as a source of money throughout life: she must never yield in her demands so as to get the maximum of what is hers by right.

But many, perhaps most, women spend their whole life in a marriage feeling they never get anything like their due. What they do get is plenty of accusations from their husbands that they are squanderers and extremely spendthrift. Against such accusations

Role formation within marriage 121

there is little proof the women can show of their own innocence, beyond confirmation from the children about their mother's whole-hearted struggle to economize, and the price levels. One of the women, Umm Ali, after twenty-two years of accusations like these, therefore decided to furnish herself with some indisputable arguments to hit back with. By becoming self-supporting and not looking after the house for her husband she could 'stand at a distance from him and observe him' (*mashya biçíd çannu batfarrag çaléh*), i.e. not be made responsible for his housekeeping expenses. She got herself a job – after strenuous effort – in a factory. The husband became furious, beat her and cracked her nose, and demanded a divorce. But when she happily agreed, he capitulated and accused her of having provoked the threat of divorce to be able to marry someone else. Her brother was brought in to mediate and told her to show patience. Umm Ali replied: 'To hell with patience. There's no point in talking about patience when the family goes without food for not only *one* day but two and three, yes, a week!' She said she had already been stupid enough to sit patiently at home for twenty years while her husband only used the home as a hotel! Then she started her job, while two teenage daughters looked after the house. This did not prove an easy way out, since with transport and working hours the working day became eleven hours long with a net income of £3.60 a month and even more work washing clothes, etc. at night. But she managed to get her proof. The household used up more money when she was away and they also lost material resources in the form of small 'loans' to neighbours who saw their chance to make little profits while the housewife was out. (They borrowed sugar, tea, and such things which they never gave back.) Moreover, it was discovered that clothes had been stolen from the cupboard, obviously by visitors. Last, but not least, it turned out that the daughters had sold various belongings, such as kitchen utensils, to get the money for household expenses. Without the mother's sources to borrow from, they saw this as their last resort.

After she had been working for four months in the factory, her husband begged her to stop, promising in front of witnesses to give her an acceptable fixed monthly amount of money. Her strategy thus turned out to be effective, but cannot easily be imitated by other women for various reasons: the labour market is flooded and an enormously strong will is required for success; public opinion condemns such strong revolt against the husband's authority, and the woman must have an exceptionally strong character to be able to ignore what people say (see p. 57: the incident about baking cakes).

It is worthwhile to note the assets at this particular woman's command. Not only does she have an unusually strong character, she also has the total loyalty of several grown-up children, she has male defenders, and places of refuge. The husband, on the other hand, has never had any female relatives to support him. His only family is that of marriage, and he is strongly attached to both children and wife.

In the later phases of marriage the in-law family becomes less difficult for the woman. The woman's family also creates less problems for the husband than before, not because they keep away more, but because the husband seems to have resigned himself to the inevitable. What he is prepared to accept as expenses on their behalf varies, however, with his power position in relation to his wife. In one case I know he went as far as accepting that his wife's sister and her five children move into his flat where nine people were living already. They occupied several of his own children's beds and ate almost entirely at his expense. This situation lasted for three months. Then the husband seemed to want to carry out his threat to move into a hotel, and his wife asked her sister to move with her children instead. My impression is that the wife at this point was so run down herself by the noise and the over-crowding, and so bitter over the money that was being lost, that she was happy to have an excuse to get rid of the relatives. To placate them she 'lent' them a double bed and some bedclothes.

We can see that as time passes the woman gradually builds up an ever stronger power position vis-à-vis her husband. It gives her greater influence over her own daily activities, a freer choice with whom to spend her time, and more control over the general affairs of the household. But it is doubtful whether this also results in a greater flow to her from her husband of the things she values most in life. She remains poor, and no doubt seems to experience throughout life that she has qualities which her husband either does not see, or does not value properly, and that she is ignored and neglected in very painful ways. But why then does she systematically build up a position which gives her increasing independence and power, and entails a mannish and assertive role (cf. the popular generalizations like 'the woman rules here', etc.) if this still does not give her the things she values the most? To understand this we shall have to consider her total situation in terms of the opportunities it provides for self-realization.

EIGHT

Self-realization in a poor environment

> 'Half of the harm that is done in this world
> Is due to people who want to feel important.
> They don't mean to do harm – but the harm does not interest them.
> Or they do not see it, or they justify it
> Because they are absorbed in the endless struggle
> To think well of themselves.'
> T. S. Eliot, *The Cocktail Party*

It is a reasonable presumption that people everywhere seek recognition from others and confirmation that they have qualities which are positive and desirable within their particular culture. Each culture has its own picture of these qualities and thus one could say that the elements which can be included in the 'self' that people want to have confirmed are culturally defined and form a smaller or larger register of possibilities or potential qualities. Some cultures encourage many different forms of self-expression and activity, whereas others impose stricter and more narrow demands on a person's standards. The culture also provides us with the frames of interpretation we use to evaluate other people's reactions to ourselves. A Norwegian's reaction to an Italian friend, for example, which he himself considers friendly, may well be interpreted by the Italian as very reserved, even cold and rejecting as understood in his frame of interpretation. The structure of the society in which we live provides us with occasions and means to realize our objectives and ourselves, but also presents us with threats of defeat in relation to rivals and competitors.

In this chapter I will try to show how the life style of the poor women in Cairo can be seen as the end product of their 'struggle to think well of themselves'. My material indicates that the form their struggle takes is affected by the fact that they are primarily seeking to *obtain* recognition from others, rather than to live up to internalized values and standards.[1]

In other words it is a question not of primarily 'being true to oneself' but rather of doing what brings recognition even if this entails 'compromising one's true self'. I shall try to show this by describing (i) how the women, in agreement with their own local culture, conceive of the picture of themselves which they want others to reflect, (ii) what possibilities and limitations they are faced with, and (iii) what they actually achieve. I shall then try to show how this type of activity on the part of many individuals creates a society which reproduces its own preconditions.

In an over-populated, overcrowded slum, most of people's lives are enacted on an open stage. As we have seen, this means that the poor in Cairo must live with the constant, pressing interference of others into their private lives, and resign themselves to the fact that practically all their defeats and failures will be publicized. In their struggle to project an admirable self-image, the women therefore have to try and counteract in one way or another the effect of the defeats they suffer from husband and others. This they do to a large extent by creating confirmatory little circles where their own value is asserted whilst other women are degraded with gossip and slander. Thus a neighbourhood is created in which people are engaged in a constant struggle to elevate themselves at the expense of others.

On the basis of Egyptian values and ideals, I could construct a synthetic image of the type of person that the woman wants to hear she is. The main ingredients would be: a humble, loyal wife, a

---

[1] This agrees with the picture of culture and personality Ammar gives in his profound analysis – see especially Chapters 6 and 10. Also see Berger (1964):

'One aspect of the cultural outlook we have been discussing is the Arab's infatuation with ideal forms; he clings to them emotionally even while he knows they are contradicted by reality. The distinction between ideal and real exists in other societies too, but there is more awareness of the gap between the two, and the ideal is more consciously held up as basis upon which to *judge* the real. Arabs confuse the two, professing to believe against reality that the ideal is carried out in conduct and is identical with practice rather than merely constituting the criterion by which practice is to be judged. A Christian missionary has told a revealing story of how he placed before an Arab audience the question as to which son in the New Testament parable (Matthew 21:28) is the better: the one who, when asked by his father to do something, replies that he will and then does not, or the son who replies that he will not and then does what his father asks. Virtually all the Arabs said the son who answered that he would was the better because, even though he did not carry out his father's wish, he showed proper respect to an ideal form of verbal acquiescence rather than a real act of obedience ("real" by Western standards).'

self-sacrificing mother, an altruistic person who never gossips and who generally never does anything that could be ethically blameworthy. None of the women seem to be striving to realize such a self in practice, and it is indeed a target beyond reach in the situation in which they live. This should be clear from the preceding chapters; as we have seen, scarce resources, the person's understanding of her own environment as expressed in the folk generalizations, and the lack of a so-called 'back stage' make the realization of such a self more or less impossible. The women instead concentrate on obtaining *social* confirmation that they *are* what their culture says they should be. It is therefore through other people's reactions, which the women themselves interpret as recognition of their own value and identity, that they try to realize themselves.

In other words, to describe self-realization in a society it is not enough to ask what ideals people there are trying to live up to. We have to examine what they actually do in real life to have their value confirmed. I believe the methodologically most satisfactory way to do this is to base the analysis on a description of actual, concrete events through which women have achieved self-confirmation, that is, where they have scored in ways that satisfied them.

One methodological problem, however, remains: how to identify successes which 'satisfied the women'. The selection must necessarily be based on the anthropologist's impressions, and reflect subjective views. But by seeing these selected events in the light of my total description of the living environment, the reader should be provided with a basis for judging the plausibility of my interpretations.

Recognition is sought from all the categories of adults who make up the woman's social world: husband, women-friends, acquaintances, relatives, in-laws, enemies and, to a certain extent, strangers. As we saw in Chapter 4, these people form a surprisingly small circle, whose membership is constantly changing. At any time there is a small inner core consisting of the individuals who are most important to the woman. The husband's unique importance has been documented – also mother's and brother's special positions. Moreover, one to three women-friends are included. Significant in all these relationships is the fact that trust dominates mistrust, and each single relationship is seen as a *total* relationship obliging the whole person. Unreservedly positive responses are expected and are very specially appreciated, and besides, the woman seems to identify with these people in the way that any of their scores are seen as scores for herself. To protect the relationships she systematically tries to interpret away clearly negative reactions with folk generalizations about manipulation: 'He/she loves me but because of manipulation he/she does this or that...' (*biyḥibbini, bass min ittaslīṭ*) is a standard formula and form of reasoning.

Figure 8(1): *Friendship and alliance*

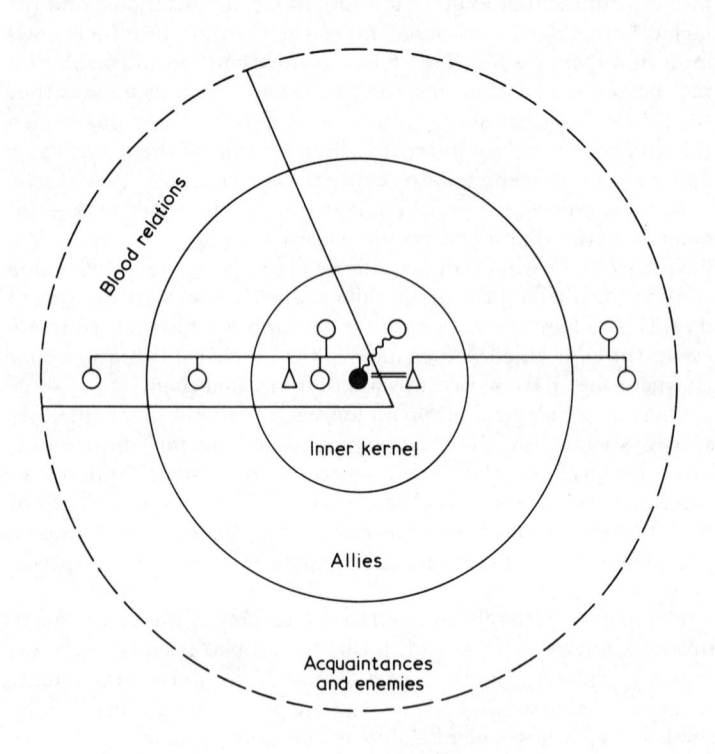

[Diagram: concentric circles labeled "Inner kernel", "Allies", "Acquaintances and enemies", with a sector marked "Blood relations"]

The other relationships which make up a woman's social world are, to a greater or lesser extent, dominated by mistrust. This affects interaction and also the frames of interpretation which the woman applies to such people's acts: folk generalizations say that they are people with 'two faces', that is, they are deceitful and hypocritical (p. 48) and do not generally wish anybody well (p. 48). As a consequence, the woman can never feel sure that their positive behaviour towards her reflects actual positive evaluations, that is, are expressions of recognition, especially since manifestations of respect such as flattery and humouring are institutionalized in the culture

(p. 139). But from these people, she is prepared to find that they do not even show her this elementary politeness, and that therefore she may also have negative reactions from them. However, such signals are not necessarily counted as lack of recognition; the woman may interpret criticism as envy from the other woman, or pettiness, and thereby reinterpret it as a positive score for herself.

By using this basic differentiation of types of fellow-humans and types of reactions, we can now identify those events which represent positive scorings for a woman.

The clearest and most unequivocal scorings are those based on control of material goods. I have already mentioned how the woman, by showing off outside her home things like new clothes, can reach a large, diffuse audience with a message of her success. The same thing happens each time she, her husband, or the children walk down the streets with new acquisitions which the door-sitters, balcony-standers, window-peepers, and passers-by quickly and selectively identify. Purchases of better foodstuffs, such as meat, fish, vegetables of a better quality, etc. likewise give positive scorings. The same is true at Ramadan, when the women bring their baking sheets to the bakeries to have their cakes baked, and everyone's attention is intensely directed towards the degree of yellowness of the other women's dough – as this is seen as an indication of the price of the butter they have used. Even the *declaration* that one plans to buy things obviously serves as a scoring and is therefore uttered in strategic situations. I have heard a woman exclaim in a loud voice: 'I shall buy a television – *and pay cash!*' as she passed her main enemy in the street. On another, similar occasion another woman advertised: 'I shall have a blouse made, the like of which has never been seen in this neighbourhood!'

When such scorings are seen as so clear and unequivocal, it is because people are unanimous that material goods are what everybody *else* wants most in life – regardless of what they say. Therefore the woman does not need a confirmatory response from her audience. She can apply the folk generalizations about envy and know that she has scored. That these frames of interpretation are general can be shown by the enemy's reflection on the statement above about the television purchase: 'Obviously she said it just to make me envious but why should I be envious. (*w'ana bakraḥ*) Don't all things come from Allah!' From the attitude about envy Umm Foad also knew that she had scored by buying fish at the market one day when the fish was expensive (see p. 46) although an acquaintance of hers advised her: 'No, by the Prophet's name, why do it today, sister, you will spend a lot of money! Wait till another day!' The undisputable recognition came when she fried the fish and the oil spat and burnt her arm: it was the evil power of envy, the evil eye.

Events which reveal material defeats are mentioned by women as the things in life of which they are most ashamed. One woman who had her furniture thrown in the street because she owed two months' rent was beside herself with despair over the wide publicity this gave to her disgrace. In order to cover up material limitations and avoid stigmatization the women make use of a series of standardized strategies: they are very careful to borrow money only from people they trust completely, and when this is impossible they borrow from people who *do not live in the same house or the same street* so that the chance of a quarrel and consequent revelation is minimized. They send the children to borrow money because they are 'too young to feel the shame'. They refuse almost in panic to receive hospitality for fear of giving the hostess a reason to say later, triumphantly: 'She didn't have enough money for food'. A series of examples have been given that show how dominant this theme is.

Another fundamentally different way to score is when a social situation is created where a woman achieves social confirmation through a favourable comparison with another. In such activities, different tactics are used as the opportunity arises. To give an example of this game I shall construct a rough typology 1-5, although the types as empirical phenomena in real life situations blend into each other.

(1) One type of scoring is achieved when another person, X, clearly gives the woman priority at the expense of a third person, Y. Such priority represents a clear recognition of this woman in front of Y. When, for example, Umm Ali's best friend, Umm Laila, comes straight from her sister to her and says: 'I'm so hungry, give me something to eat', she gives Umm Ali a declaration of trust she has not even dared give her sister – and Umm Ali feels she is given total recognition. When a girl's fiancé used to come directly to the house of his fiancée's mother during his leave, before going to his own mother, the fiancée and her mother saw this as a great triumph. But the greatest victory a woman can ever experience in this way is when a husband or brother prefers her to her sister-in-law. Umm Mohammed felt this when Ahmed said to his sister in front of his wife: 'I have to feed the children Allah has given me before feeding yours.' Next time it was the sister's turn to score when Ahmed took the initiative to let her move in with them and swore 'by his eyes' (*min 'éni*) that he would carry her on his hands and feet and throw out his wife if she made any trouble. But the

ultimate triumph was Umm Mohammed's the following day, when she managed to provoke a quarrel so that the sister-in-law was thrown out, while Ahmed watched without intervening. Similar empirical examples have already been given (see p. 111). The value of such scorings also depend on the strength of the woman's rivalry with Y, and the importance of X to her. The most important occasions of all will therefore be when the woman feels that her husband prefers her to the sister-in-law.

(2) If such a comparison is not to the advantage of the woman, pride will force her to break off the relationship, unless the unfaithfulness can be explained away as the result of manipulation. It is typical here that in a case involving people in her inner circle, the woman will initiate a frenetic campaign to prove how he, she or they have been manipulated. We have already seen such cases in the relationship between engaged couples (p. 88) married couples, (p. 98) and father-daughter, (p. 95) and for relations between women-friends and brothers and sisters, it is also common. For example, when Ahmed let his sister be thrown out by his wife, she rushed straight to her sister and complained about her cruel sister-in-law, whereas the brother was emphasized as only good and kind and manipulated by his wife. Even the most unequivocal personal actions will be seen by a woman in this light. Once, when 'the children had been fighting', Umm Foad, seven months pregnant, had to take refuge on the top floor because her elder brother hammered on the front door in a rage, a knife in his hand to attack her — while her old, eighteen-stone mother was pressing against the door from the inside. Even then the brother was wholly without blame because 'his wife had manipulated him'.

(3) Scoring over another woman can also be achieved by other people agreeing with the woman's account of a course of events involving herself and Y, or of comparisons between herself and Y in similar situations. In such accounts people in the inner circle can also take the woman's place, since scorings for them are taken vicariously as scorings for herself. The story-teller always presents herself as the ethically perfect and Y as wholly to blame. Conversations are literally seething with stories like this. They seem to me both significant and insignificant, long and short, and varying in content from day to day. One day Umm Aleyya gave this version of the moral corruption of her son-in-law's sister, Umm Ali: 'Just imagine, she did not invite Ahmed to the reading of the Koran for her daughter because she was angry that Ahmed had refused to lend her £30 she owed after having wasted it on *her* children!' The following day the story was: 'She didn't invite Ahmed because he had criticized the dreadful methods they used to get hold of the

bridegroom!' Ahmed's version was: 'They invited me for Wednesday next week – not yesterday!' And Umm Ali's household gave the impression of expecting Ahmed for hours before the celebration: 'We *have* invited him but he's probably angry because I criticized his behaviour with Karima' (see p. 129).

Other typical examples are: a woman reproached her sister for being so greedy that she sold a washtub to her for 80p and then came to borrow it each time she needed it! Another told about an acquaintance – on the same day enmity exploded between them – who had stolen her clock from under her mattress. Only when the woman deliberately said that she would go to a truthsayer to find the thief, did the thief come back with the clock with the excuse that the woman's three-year-old daughter had given it to her. A third described how she herself always rushes out to defend her cousin's children when others hit them, whereas the cousin stands arms akimbo, watching, while others hit her children. An extremely important and frequently mentioned Y in these stories is the woman's husband. The woman thereby marks the distance from him which is essential for her to emerge as an independent, morally elevated individual untarnished by his failure.

My understanding of these stories is that they function as myths for the people. They are legitimizing versions of existing relationships – and their truth value is completely secondary or unimportant. This interpretation is based on two types of observations: that women will (a) describe one single course of events differently according to their changing relations to Y and (b) accept unflustered any suggestions that their own versions are wrong or contradictory. One event can serve as an example of this: a woman was talking about her sister's selfish and greedy character: 'Their cupboards are *full* of clothes – lots that they never use – and they never give away old things to us who need them.' The following day the story was: 'They only have what they need themselves, it's only this year that they've become better off.' (And as I provoked her by asking what they do with old clothes) . . . 'No, they haven't got any old clothes. Their clothes never get old, since they need all they have . . . It's only this year that they've become better off.'

In other words, as I understand these stories they are primarily an attempt by the woman to describe the quality of her social relations and for X to confirm or, in the worst of cases, deny his/her relation to the woman, according to whether he or she accepts the story or not.

(4) In other forms of gossip the favourable comparison is implicit for the woman. Unlike the gossip I have already mentioned, the

Self-realization in a poor environment 131

speaker or people close to her do not appear in these stories. I have already (p. 58) developed my interpretation of the gossip in the poor quarter primarily as a framework for the woman's self-presentation rather than as diffuse informal sanctions against others, and I have analysed examples showing this. Therefore I shall now mention only two cases: Umm Foad talking about a neighbour, Umm Sami, who is so poor she has had to send one child away: 'She has lots of money but that doesn't show in her furniture, because she *eats* up her money. She buys meat and kilos of water melon every day! It's a shame! (*çéb*). She ought to spend that money trying to look decent!' Umm Gamal about her sister, Umm Anwar: 'She has lots of money because she gives the children awful food and never lets them have their stomachs' fill. It's a shame! Everyone needs nutritious food.'

(5) Last but not least, much of the woman's effort to have her self-image confirmed takes the form of explicit self-praise: suddenly, in the middle of a conversation, the hostess may exclaim: 'Look, how people love us because we are such good people!' (*iḥna nás çumara*). Other typical refrains in conversation are: '... because I'm so intelligent', (*madám fi moxx, madám moxxi kibīr*) '... because I love people so much' (*madám fi insaniyya*), etc. Events like this one are also typical: a woman showed a friend and me some photographs, one of which was of a very fat woman, and praised herself: 'I'm just right, neither too fat nor too thin, aren't I?' Umm Aleyya, who begs money from her son-in-law almost every day, boasted in front of both him and others that she, who is so needy, will never ask Ahmed for anything at all — she doesn't even *ask* what the daughter and son-in-law do with their money — that is entirely their business!

The types of scorings described above all take place in social situations where people meet in a friendly atmosphere, and they depend on the participants giving each other social confirmation. But there are other situations which offer obvious opportunities for scoring, through direct confrontation with enemies, and without an immediate need for social confirmation. When the woman confronts an enemy, she can either abuse her, disgrace her, and/or resort to violence. Many of the same themes as those included in the scorings above appear in such confrontations:

'Where is the 70p you borrowed?'
'I'm better than you because I eat better, drink better, and dress better than you!'
'You were a bride with nothing but a bag — I had both furniture and money!'
'My husband is better dressed than yours!'

'I'm better than you, you illiterate!'
'You daughter of servants!'
'I've never left my husband like you!'
'May Allah curse/destroy you!'
'Who are the whores you rub shoulders with?'

In order to provoke confrontations women sometimes break into each other's flats. A more refined type of break-in to disgrace an enemy happened when Umm Mohammed broke into the flat of her then enemy, Umm Hussein, during her absence and stood by the window shouting abuse at Umm Hussein's friend and cousin and her own enemy, Umm Fathma, across the street. She thereby managed to give the impression that Umm Hussein had allied herself with Umm Mohammed against her own cousin, and so broke up their friendship. She also managed to get the cousin to tell Umm Hussein's in-laws that Umm Mohammed had been 'invited' into the flat, which the in-laws had specifically forbidden Umm Hussein to do, and so release a storm of rage against Umm Hussein. It didn't help that Umm Hussein protested that the 'visit' was a break-in. Suspicion is so great that no one would believe her.

Actual violence is also frequent (see Chapter 1), against both people and belongings. The same Umm Hussein, for example, had to move her television set away from the window and wrap it in a wool rug to protect it from stones and filth hailing in through the window from the roof of the cousin's house across the street. Scorings from violence are highly valued, e.g. the woman who would be pleased to pay a £100 fine (p. 67).

These forms of scoring are all part of the game women play in order to assert and have confirmed their own value and identity in their environment. This game involves both material resources and non-material qualities, such as recognition and criticism. In many societies in the world we know of processes by which people *transform* material resources into non-material forms of value, such as for example, social recognition. This is often called *conversion* in anthropological literature. Such conversion in the shape of generosity and hospitality is certainly well recognized and valued in Egyptian culture, and is expressed by an insistent demand that one should receive what is offered by *itfaḍḍal* – please. In spite of that ideal, however, the reality among the poor is strictly the contrary.

During Ramadan there is a ceremonial exchange of cakes. If a woman receives less than she gives, her reaction is not that she has scored materially but that she has been *offended*. And for a long time afterwards one may accuse the other: 'I gave a box, you just a plate!' When gifts are exchanged on ritual occasions one carefully avoids giving first to a person whom one suspects is not likely to give in return. One woman who honoured another with a gift of meat and rice and was given 20p in return became so bitter that she admitted having seized on the first possible occasion to curse the other: 'May your husband die!' Another was furious with her stepmother, who had come to visit her for three days and 'wanted to eat all the time – eightpence-worth of milk, sugar and tea just for breakfast! And she didn't even bring a gift when she came!' One woman in this neighbourhood, Umm Anwar, who has long been suspected of murder, has chosen quite a different strategy and by giving away homemade cakes tries to buy the benevolence of Allah. She knows that the receivers will criticize her behind her back: 'She ought to buy food for her children instead!' But she herself believes that Allah will love her because 'she loves people' (*bithibb innās*).

Nor can this be interpreted as an investment in status symbols. The material goods people acquire are not selected just to be shown off. They are necessities which, in the objective sense of the word, always come too little and too late. It may be a pair of new shoes every two instead of every three years, a new divan because the old one is collapsing, etc. But because they all live under the same conditions of deprivation, each new acquisition will, to a certain extent, serve as a status symbol.

The main thing is to *maximize control* of the resources available. To secure this control one seeks to commit oneself to as few reciprocal obligations as possible. I have even observed instances when women have rejected gifts on ritual occasions to avoid the obligation of returning the gift on a similar occasion in the giver's family. To retain maximum control is precarious, because one's material resources are threatened by the rights of relatives and in-laws. They have a right to *take* things they want or feel they need more than the woman herself. The only way to protect one's assets is therefore to hide them: one woman hid her bracelets to prevent her brothers and sisters, if they should be in acute need, from demanding them. Another, who did *not* hide her engagement gifts, had to give them to her mother-in-law when she came to ask for them. One woman who proudly showed some little pictures of her children rushed to hide them under the mattress when she heard footsteps outside the flat; she was afraid it might be her sister-in-law and that she might claim the pictures if she saw them. Another who *was* caught by her father's sister whilst showing someone her new nightdress reportedly had the nightdress taken away from her with the words: 'I'll take this as a wedding gift to my daughter.'[1]

[1] To protect his material assets from such demands, a man about to go to Kuwait to work stated that he would only be sending back money – no goods.

In other words, one has to *have* and *possess* material objects, not use them or convert them socially. This does not mean that conversions are non-existent. The most important occasions which I witnessed during my field work are the following. Umm Hussein paid £2 in rent to enable her cousin and her husband to move from a distant poor quarter in Cairo to the house next door to her own. This conversion of a considerable amount of money to a social relation must be seen from the point of view of her weak strategic position (p. 113): she meant to gain an ally to support her against her husband and neighbours. Instead, the cousin soon went over to the enemy and became an endless source of new conflicts (pp. 55, 138 and 52-4) and the conversion brought on a loss.

Laila's aunt brought presents from Kuwait, worth £7-£8 according to Egyptian standards, to Laila and her family. She was hoping to achieve a marriage between her son and Laila, and when this failed she demanded her gifts back and gave them to Soad's aunt and enemy, Umm Anwar, her new ally.

A woman whose husband returned home from Libya gave her two women-friends a slip and a pair of stockings. This, however, only led to bitter feelings in the one who had the less expensive present, the stockings.

Small conversions of material resources into hospitality also take place at times. A typical example of this occurred when Umm Ali managed to get her enemy's allies in from the street and then secretly sent her children out to buy three bottles of Pepsi-Cola, which she offered to her guests. They refused almost hysterically to drink it, tried to get the children to drink it instead, and were obviously 'caught' when they failed (2p represents such a large amount that no guest could possibly commit the crime of wasting it). It was equally obvious that, as Umm Ali managed to engage them in conversation, they enjoyed the drink increasingly. Such manoeuvres can have a double objective: they can be the beginning or the confirmation of an alliance, and at the same time, the hostess is provided with ammunition for possible future slander and confrontations. People are so aware of this danger that they will often panic and rush to the door the moment the hostess threatens to serve them something.

With such conversions so seldom leading to the desired result, the opportunist quality of inter-human relations is further revealed. And it takes very little before the receiver is somehow offended by the giver and therefore feels completely excused from any demands of reciprocity. Conversion therefore does not emerge as an alternative pattern to *having* and *possessing* material things. This is taken for granted to the extent that people do not even take offence when the ideal of hospitality is neglected. One hostess had bought a portion of grapes for me specially. When I only ate very little she sat down and ate the rest herself in front of the other guests – and no one seemed embarrassed.

The control of material goods is in other words the trump card in this game for social recognition. Why does a poor population in acute need of material resources choose to concentrate all efforts on such a value scale? The answer is partly found in aspects of shared Egyptian culture and partly in the ecology of life in the back streets.

In all strata of Egyptian society, a person's value seems to be measured to an overwhelming extent by the amount of material goods he/she owns. In their interaction with others, people will therefore primarily concentrate on constantly acquiring larger amounts of this value. I shall illustrate this with two examples. A Swedish charity organization sent parcels of toys for distribution to Egyptian children's homes. The official receiving the present then insisted on first choosing the nicest toys for his own children. And on one occasion when I needed the signature of a Coptic priest to take out, custom-free, a parcel containing old clothes collected by a Norwegian woman specially for my poor friends, everyone I consulted could tell me that the priest would demand at least half of the clothes for himself as a token of my appreciation. The problem was solved by the American University paying the £10 customs duty.

Poor people's interaction with representatives of the Establishment is based on similar premises. Bribes flow unilaterally upwards in society, yet no stable patron-client relations are established. In other words, bribes give only temporary and *ad hoc* protection. In their contact with administration, hospitals, etc. the poor will constantly experience the stigma of poverty and must acquiesce to being treated accordingly. (e.g. Ahmed who could not get a doctor's certificate in spite of a bribe, p. 160). How aware they are of this connection can be seen from the arguments used to justify Gamal's need for a new sweater: 'or else no one will want to be his friend'.

An under-privileged, poor population has little opportunity to dissociate itself from such a dominant standard. What is more, material goods have certain qualities which make them particularly suited for the purposes of the poor: (i) They are tangible. In a community where most relations are based on the premise that no one wishes anybody else well, it is definitely an advantage not to be captive of the benevolence of others but to have control oneself of the source of social recognition. (ii) They reach a large audience.

Women are very restricted in the social contacts they can have; there are few circles or social occasions where they can interact with many people. But material goods can be exhibited regardless of social relations or occasions. The streets one passes through are populated by women who are trained selectively to identify new acquisitions and who form a *large* audience. The constant talk about prices creates a mutual understanding amongst the people about relative material values. (iii) They are finely adjusted. The rivalry between women takes place between two at a time, and since they are all on about the same level, even small acquisitions – nuances of quality of a blanket, etc. – will represent important scorings.

Moreover, these people see material goods as the key to happiness itself. They have the personal experience and general insight that their poverty is the source of all their misery and unhappiness. Their idea of the good life has material things as its essence, as is shown by a woman's account of the Sudan, the work place of her nephew, a well-known actor: 'The Sudan is *very* good. Mutton cost very little, meat is cheap, sweets are cheap, there are good schools. He will be *very* happy there.' In other words, material goods are simultaneously both the most effective means to get others to reflect a flattering self-image and the basis of the realization of all their dreams and desires.

It is essential to point out that each woman will claim that it is *all the others* who measure people by their material assets, whereas *she herself* measures them by their moral qualities. *Others* will be angry and offended when material deprivation prevents one from fulfilling obligations to them, such as giving gifts on ritual occasions, whereas she herself is understanding and forgiving. She herself will love those who accept her hospitality whereas others feel hatred in their hearts.

She also considers people's manoeuvring to harm others as an expression of envy or a struggle for material superiority. When one woman tried to destroy the friendship between Umm Mohammed and Umm Hussein both of them saw this as an expression of envy because they have television sets and she has not. When Abdullah's mother tried to destroy the friendship between her son and wife and Ahmed and wife, Ahmed and his wife saw the motive as being 'fear that Abdullah might give them things'. When Abdu's mother tried to destroy the engagement between her son and Umm Gamal's daughter, Umm Gamal saw the motive as being 'fear that Abdu might give her cakes'. I could give innumerable examples of this.

However, the women constantly reveal inadvertently that they themselves – just like all the others – give priority to a material scale of values and compete on this basis. Umm Foad's one comment on a lengthy public parading of the neighbour's daughter's bridal equipment was: 'She hasn't got a side-board! – and the stuffing in the mattress is awful!' Umm Mohammed warmly supported Umm Hussein, her best friend, in front of Umm Hussein's father in a long conversation aimed at criticizing Umm Hussein's husband, Abdullah, for giving money to the wife and children of his imprisoned brother. But when the father went further and wanted to claim this money for Umm Hussein, she suddenly did a volte-face: 'No, no, in the name of the Prophet, Abdullah doesn't let her go without *anything*! He gives her *everything* she needs in the way of money and clothes. Her only problem is that her in-laws won't leave her alone!' I could give many examples of a similar kind.

Thus people conceive of two quite different aspects of the person: one material and one moral. Where they themselves are concerned, they experience a clear discrepancy between these standards: they are poor but morally elevated. When they evaluate others, however, they do not apply the standards to identify different aspects of the person but to judge each person as a whole. This enables them to practice what is their main stategy: to devalue a person who scores on one scale by means of the other scale – or rather, by using whatever opportunity to criticize is nearest at hand, whether a criticism of material standards or of moral virtue. For example, the moral victory constituted by a marriage is reduced by criticism of the quality of the dowry; material scoring is reduced by criticism of behaviour, and a morally praiseworthy act is cancelled out by reference to an immoral act. How typical such criticism is of a normal flow of conversation, I shall show with an excerpt from my field notes.

Umm Foad:
'We don't believe in the evil eye. Many people do but we don't. And Umm Said doesn't [her sister] – she used to show off Said [her son] although he was white and fat. But Umm Manal! We never dare say that her children are pretty, we say: "Those are ugly." And the neighbours on the first floor! When one of their children was ill, they told me it was due to the evil eye of the ones without children on the second floor. But there are good people as well, Umm Hosni who lives nextdoor to us, she will *ask* Laila [Umm Foad's daughter] to hold her little one when she finds her standing by the door, and she herself is busy washing. But she is

very rich, she owns a house with two floors and won't let them because she says they don't need to and she doesn't want any trouble. Even so, she'll never give us poor any used clothes! She'll *sell* them for a penny or two! *Nobody* here wants anyone else to have anything!'

How are the circles for these conversations formed – that is, how are the opportunities created by which the woman obtains social recognition from a favourable comparison with another (see items (1)-(4) above)? As mentioned above, each woman surrounds herself with an inner circle of persons who are freely accessible to her, and whom she knows will be interested in and accept her stories. Apart from this, she can when she likes reach a much larger network of people: the fact that each woman has a number of enemies in the neighbourhood means that anyone who wants to degrade her has a pre-established field of potential allies. Enemies are always on the look-out for ever new occasions to vent their bitterness and condemnation of each other. When a conflict is acute – after a confrontation – the woman will therefore visit her enemy's enemies, or they her, and thus new circles are formed where allies meet in order to pursue their common interest for as long as the conflict is acute. During this degradation process, the allies, as well as the people in the woman's inner circle, whole-heartedly and unconditionally support each other's versions. The effect of these strategies is that each conflict spreads through the neighbourhood in the shape of new alliances. This can be illustrated by a few selected examples: (i) Umm Hussein and her in-laws had not been on speaking terms for a whole year (see p. 113) but this condition changed the day both of them became involved on the same side in a conflict with Umm Mohammed's family. (ii) When enmity broke out between Umm Hussein and her cousin (see pp. 53-5) the cousin's first act was to rush to Umm Hussein's arch enemies, the mother-in-law and sister-in-law. This new situation was clearly demonstrated. I sat by the window together with Umm Hussein as Umm Hussein's brother-in-law went by. The cousin shouted in an ingratiating voice from her roof: 'Good evening, Aby Hosham.' 'Good evening, Umm Fathma. Is there anything I can do for you?' 'No, thank you. May God be with you.' Similar amiability was repeated on later occasions. (iii) When the engagement of Umm Mohammed's sister, Aziza, was broken off, this immediately led to intense socializing between her family and the former bridegroom's sister's sister-in-law. (iv) Mustafa's wife and mother were not on speaking terms for several months. They lived in the same flat, but the situation

Figure 8(2)

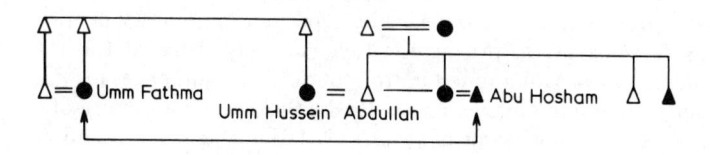

Figure 8(3)

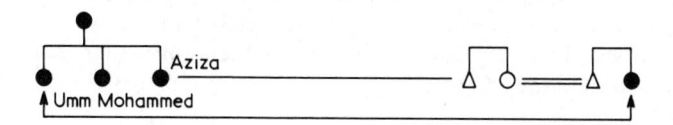

changed on the day when his father, said to be manipulated by the children of his first marriage, tried to throw Mustafa and his family out on the street. Structurally equivalent situations also appear in the preceding pages, see for example p. 111. They are *very* frequent in this community.

Interaction in these confirmatory little circles is subject to strict, categorical rules of behaviour. All the people present have to confirm each other's statements and stories, and humour each other in all situations. This is the essence of politeness and respect and any deviation from it is an insult. How strict these rules actually are may be seen from the consequences that ensue when they are broken: (i) One morning when Umm Gamal was in a very bad mood after having quarrelled with her husband, Umm Aleyya came round to watch television. Umm Gamal hurriedly tried to compose herself but she obviously failed, for Umm Aleyya was deeply offended: she remained standing by the door telling Umm Gamal off for receiving her in such a foul mood when she came to see whether there was any entertainment on television. Umm Gamal was furious; she took her blind little daughter and held her in front of Umm Aleyya: 'Are you surprised that I'm unhappy, having three like this!' (She has three blind children.) The daughter, Laila, was equally furious: 'What do you want us to do – roll out our telly on a red carpet for you?' The end of it all was three months of the two families not being on speaking terms. (ii) A little while before the confrontation between Umm Mohammed and her sister-in-law, Karima, Umm Mohammed was showing some photographs of herself to a couple of women-friends. She gave them one each and Karima asked for one but Umm Mohammed refused her, on the pretext that she had already promised some other people. On several occasions during the following days I heard Karima condemn Umm Mohammed in front of different audiences for this impertinence. One may ask oneself why she wanted a picture of a woman she cannot stand anyway. (iii) Laila asked her friend to come to the shop with her to buy a piece of needlework. She chose one and said to her friend: 'This is nice, isn't it?' The friend replied quite truthfully that she preferred another. Laila was then very offended. 'Why do you say that everything I have is ugly?' 'But you asked me to say what I thought, and I am older than you, so you should do what I tell you,' the other one replied. Four months of not being on speaking terms ensued. (iv) One of several pieces of soap

Figure 8(4)

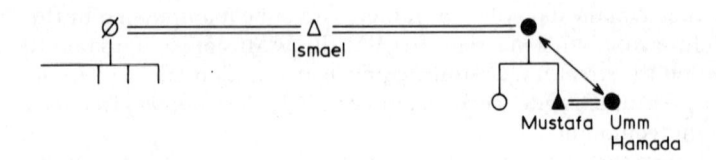

```
      ∅ ═══════════ △ ══════════════ ●
                   Ismael             │
      ┌──┴──┐                  ┌──────┤
      │     │                  ○    ▲═●
                              Mustafa Umm
                                     Hamada
```

was missing from Umm Hussein's cupboard, and to find out whether there had been thieves there, she asked Umm Mohammed whether perhaps Umm Hussein's little girl might have given it to her. Umm Mohammed was so offended that Umm Hussein swears that never again when something is missing from the flat will she dare ask Umm Mohammed if she has seen it. (v) Umm Gamal proudly showed her sister, Umm Anwar, her new dress. Umm Anwar remarked: 'It's ugly on you.' Umm Gamal was so unhappy that she cut up the dress and made clothes for the children from the material. In spite of this I overheard her repeatedly telling other groups that her sister's remark had only been made in envy. Applying that interpretation to the remark, she could have kept the dress as a positive scoring. But at the same time the sister belonged to the inner circle where confirmation is expected, and therefore Umm Gamal was doubtful and concerned that the dress perhaps was ugly. In other words, even material scorings become precarious within the inner circle. (vi) Umm Foad told Umm Ali that the neighbour on the ground floor was slandering her (Umm Ali). Umm

Self-realization in a poor environment 141

Ali let Umm Foad finish her story. But as soon as she had left, Umm Ali sent one of her children after her to say that it was shameful to go around gossiping like that. Enmity ensued. (vii) A friend, A, was in trouble for having said something ambiguous about her friend, B, to a third person, C. A then went to B and admitted what she had done. B was very unhappy and made this comment in front of me: 'Her greatest mistake was not to speak to C about what she did, but to tell me that she had done so.' The last two examples reveal a new aspect of the rules of interaction in the confirmatory circles. The participants must not detract from anything of value to each other, and they must not present each other with any negative scoring but exclusively praise each other and support each other's self-image.

The conversations in these circles, as I have shown in items (i)-(v) aim at slandering and condemning other people, while all those present are praised. The moral scale of value applied to degrade others has in many ways the character of an ideology of honour. It specifies obligations and ideals which people are supposed to fulfil and uses concepts such as shame (*çéb*) and face (*wishsh*). But this ideology of honour seems to differ from the concept of honour found in the Mediterranean countries and among Middle Eastern tribes. For the latter the ideology of honour is described as a set of standards which a person must fulfil to maintain his self-respect (Musil 1928; Dickson 1949). In the Mediterranean version it is a question of protecting the family's dark secrets, so that its image to the outside world will be honourable (Peristiani 1964). In this poor quarter, on the contrary, the ideology of honour seems to function primarily as a standard to justify or validate criticism and condemnation of others. It formulates a set of categorical and unlimited obligations which lack any existential anchorage: nobody can live up to them, and beyond the confirmatory circles nobody takes the woman's actual situation into consideration when applying it to her actions. But such an ideology is perfect for revealing defects in others. It thus becomes something we hold up *against them* and only in a very indirect and secondary manner will it serve as a standard for ourselves.

Let me first give an example of the first link of this argument: that the ideology works against others rather than for us. (i) Umm Aleyya condemns her son-in-law's sister for begging money from him. All members of the group hearing this criticism know that she herself constantly and indefatigably begs money both from him, her brother, and her half-brother (see p. 131). (ii) Umm Gamal criticizes her sister-in-law for not being satisfied and making do with the money her husband gives her (p. 57). All listeners know that marital conflicts on the same theme are very frequent in her own home. (iii) Umm Ali is angry with her nephew for visiting her brother Ahmed and not her. She is the enemy of the nephew's *sister*, not him, so he ought to come. She herself, however, did not go to her cousin's wedding, 'because he had quarrelled with Ahmed'.

However, indirectly and secondarily, the ideology of honour also serves as a standard for one's own actions: we know that *others*, to point out our shortcomings, hold the same kind of categorical, unattainable ideals up *against us*. How does the knowledge of such activities on the part of other women affect the woman's efforts to project an admirable self-image? What rules of conduct does she adhere to, and what results do they have?

Again, I would like to develop this argument stage by stage, and progressively document it with case material. The woman's problem is her knowledge that her actions will be commented on in circles from which she is excluded. The members of those groups will follow a stereotyped pattern: they use fragments of information greedily compiled, and with an eye to their audience, surround these fragments with the most unfavourable framework that they can hit upon. I do *not* claim that this is a conscious manoeuvre. People work with the information they have and the understanding of human nature that they have – formulated in the folk generalizations. The interpretations they apply to actions are both obvious and natural to them.

Thus, when Umm Hussein's cousin had broken open the door of Umm Hussein's flat and seen the clothes which she and Umm Mohammed were just trying on, she 'knew' that they had stolen the clothes from a sack I had brought earlier on that day. I tried in vain to prove to her that this was not so: I had *given* the clothes to Umm Mohammed and Umm Hussein. But the cousin was impossible to convince: 'You didn't see it, of course, they hid them under the divan and the bed and the cupboard when you were not looking. They took a lot of clothes.'

Alternatively, one or more participants lie, thereby providing new information which can be treated in a similar way: I would like to give one example of this – an occasion involving myself, where I thus can be quite sure of the truth. One day when Abdullah was on his way to work, he met his brother-in-law in the street. The brother-in-law told him that Umm Hussein's cousin had come to them crying, saying I had come to her to say: 'Your cousin, Umm Hussein, is not nice, she is foul – she brought Umm Mohammed and Fahima (her two friends) and let them *empty* the sack of clothes

– they took all the best clothes, and you had to take the ugliest ones which remained.' This story worried Abdullah greatly. He didn't go to work, returned home and waited for me to come so that he could sort out the matter. In my privileged position I could bring in a witness to prove that the story was a lie – in the person of the cousin's husband. This put Abdullah at peace. But none of the local participants would have been able to prove the truth like that and so eliminate the suspicion. And Umm Hussein's in-laws probably believe to this day that the cousin's version is the true one.

In other words, what is produced are myths expressing and confirming collective ideas about the character of the woman in question. Her problem in any attempt to affect this myth-creation is that there is no way in which she can control the perspective which others apply to her action. This limitation is a direct result of the demand that all those who are friends have to humour each other. Consequently, no versions can be corrected by any possible information the listeners may possess, and no objective arguments of plausibility can serve as a brake on the person telling the story. But precisely because the stories express collective views, the composition of the group will set limits to the image of the person that is drawn. Thus different groups will use different unfavourable frameworks of interpretation, and as a result, beyond the circles where the woman herself is a member, she can never control the interpretation of her own acts. Let me show this with a few examples. (i) Soad went to her friend to say: 'I have 25p – let me have your daughter photographed.' On the way to the photographer the child fell asleep and Soad returned her to her mother telling her to bring her again the following day. But neither mother nor child appeared. Soad saw this as proof that her act had been misinterpreted because 'people had talked'. (ii) Mustafa's sister, Amina, came one evening to see her mother and father, brother, and sister-in-law who all live in the same flat (they have separate rooms). I was there and observed that her father hardly said hello when she came; after a little while he went out. The conversation that ensued was mainly criticism of him: 'He only cares for the children of his first marriage. He doesn't even buy clothes for his own wife – that's up to her son (from a previous marriage). He goes to see Amina only a couple of times a month, but he goes to see Zenab, the wife of his son Raggab (living next door to Amina) every single day. He never buys anything for the children of his new wife.'

The following day, Umm Gamal could tell that Amina had been *invited* to her father's house for supper the previous day. 'None of us have ever been invited to him for a meal. But he keeps sending food

Figure 8(5)

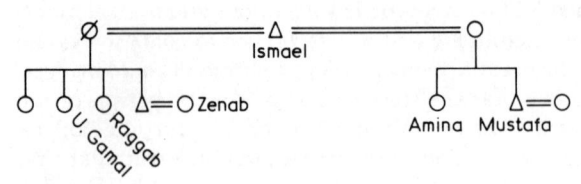

```
    ∅ ════════ △ ════════ ○
              Ismael
   ┌──┬──┬──┐              ┌────┐
   ○  ○  ○  △=○Zenab       ○    △=○
   U. Gamal                Amina Mustafa
      Raggab
```

over to Amina. He *only* cares about the children of his present wife, buys clothes for both Mustafa and his wife, while Raggab sometimes has to go to bed without food even...' I asked her how she knew about the invitation. 'We've heard about it from people' (*Simiçma min barra*). (iii) Umm Mohammed's younger sister, Gamilia, sometimes used to come and see Umm Hussein and sit with her in the evening. Then she started to come more and more often. Umm Hussein got worried, fearing that the reason was an interest on the girl's side in her husband's younger brother, Hosni, who lives in the same flat. But she dared neither tell Umm Mohammed of her suspicion nor refuse the girl access to her flat, because both would probably be seen as an offence. When the catastrophe occurred, and the girl's feelings were revealed, all Umm Mohammed's family condemned her for having *asked* Gamila to come inside every night to play ludo with her – and thus having made the infatuation possible.

All these different forms of interpretation, criticism, lying, and slander are summarized by the poor themselves in their concept of 'people's talk' (*kalám innás*) the powerful social institution which threatens everyone in the same unpredictable fashion everywhere. It is 'people's talk' which most thoroughly can destroy a woman's efforts at self-presentation, and it is 'people's talk' which she must constantly do battle against. So what means can she find to protect herself?

The following episode tells us part of the answer: Umm Mohammed had gone on a trip to the country, she was to stay away until the following day and meanwhile her mother looked after the flat. Laila came round to see Umm Muhammed. 'Sit down and wait,' the mother said. 'Umm Mohammed has gone out shopping but she'll soon be back.' After a couple of hours, Laila gave up waiting.

Umm Mohammed's mother here practised the only effective strategy against people's talk: information control. It is impossible to tell *how* she feared that the fragment of information 'Umm Mohammed has gone to the country for the day' might be misinterpreted and used against her, but it's obvious that she did have fears. The defensive method she applied is the only one available to the woman, and it is therefore practised as a general strategy. For example: Umm Gamal avoids greeting her father when she sees him on his balcony across the road, fearing that people will say she flirts with male students who also live across the road.

Umm Said tells people that her sister came to see her when she had had a baby, although the sister did not come at all. She is afraid people may talk, although it is quite common for sisters not to appear on such occasions.

Umm Ali's reply to a neighbour's question about why she does not buy butane gas is that she is afraid the children might burn themselves on it. The truth is, she cannot afford it.

Umm Ali's daughter, Zoba, dares not go out with her fiancé after the reading of the Koran, because 'people don't know yet [that the Koran has been read] and they will talk.' Umm Hamada dares not cook for her father-in-law because, if he falls ill, she fears people may she she has poisoned him.

Laila's aunt tells people that her daughter's bridegroom paid £100 as a bride-price, although he did not, in fact, pay anything at all, but the daughter loved him and the mother herself could afford to buy her furniture. If people hear that he did not pay anything, they will say: 'They accepted anyone just to get her married.'

Umm Gamal will not let anyone into her kitchen when she cooks, because she fears they might say: 'They didn't have any meat, and the tomatoes were rotten.'

Umm Sami, who does not have any relations, dared not allow two of his friends wanting to help to come and see her after her husband's death, because 'people will talk'. Several women used the example of Umm Soad to show me how truly evil people's talk can be. She had no relatives in the neighbourhood and was ignored completely by her husband, who later divorced her. When she went to see her father, she had to carry her two little children to the bus. A young boy in the neighbourhood helped her with this, and before she had time to wink, people were saying that this boy was the father of her youngest child.

In this way, the defensive manoeuvring spreads all around, and permeates life. People's talk becomes the all-embracing terror which only very few can resist to any extent. Everyone complains about the lack of freedom which results but feels powerless against it. In their efforts to project an admirable self-image and to achieve social recognition in their local community, women consequently make use of a few dominant strategies: (i) they cling to the material resources they have; (ii) they dissociate themselves from the contamination of the husband's material failure and lack of love by concentrating on independent self-presentation; (iii) they degrade each other by criticizing each other's behaviour according to an ideal moral value scale or ideology of honour; (iv) they form confirmatory little circles where they can boast about themselves without being contradicted; (v) they practise the utmost caution – in a hopeless physical environment – in their handling of all personal information; (vi) they limit their social contacts to a very restricted circle; (vii) they humour each other to avoid giving offence.

What kind of self-realization is this? The striking thing about this life is how extremely it concentrates on the handling of information, and not on the formation and realization of an inner identity through action. Although people have a potential model for the latter in the form of the ideology of honour, a strategy aiming at fulfilling it would fail completely due to the suspicion, mistrust, and people's talk which permeate the environment. Each personal act can be taken out of context, given new meanings, and condemned. Therefore people cannot expect to be rewarded with social recognition for honourable deeds. Instead, they have to seek confirmation from others, through self-presentation in the shadow of *kalám innás*. The logically most simple solution to the difficulties of information management is to restrict information through social isolation. The women are quite aware of this, and the common reaction to great disappointment in friendship is an oath to avoid any contact with neighbours in the future. After all the difficulties between Umm Hussein and Umm Mohammed, an acquaintance of Umm Hussein's advised her to do exactly like herself, isolate herself in the flat and spend her time taking out and putting back the contents of her cupboard! But women have a great need for company. To them, being alone is torture, and such resolutions are shortlived. Only one woman in the sample has chosen isolation, and is successful in the sense that she is the only one I have not heard any slander about – she lives in her miserable flat, has no friends, avoids trouble with the neighbours by keeping her children indoors, and with a husband who works overtime to ten o'clock at night each day, she must eat all her meals alone. The only person she ever sees is her sister who lives in a better street some distance away. All the other women devote themselves to frantic efforts to build a platform of a combination of items (i)-(vii). Thus they appear as relatively independent, domineering women – very different from what is probably their wish and ideal – to be like a loved and protected canary in a golden cage.

Self-realization in a poor environment 147

When all women pursue such activities for self-presentation and defence, the end product is the very environment which constrains their self-expression and causes their plight. The back streets become a *hostile* environment to the individual. Because *everybody* is *always* actively undermining *somebody* else, people's talk flourishes, all social relations are threatening and precarious, and the folk generalizations that people are false and deceitful, and never want anything good for each other, are created and confirmed. Thus the neighbourhood reproduces its characteristic social organization: small, divisive coalitions and enmities in a sea of strangers; unstable, scattered circles of acquaintances in spite of limited geographical mobility; a low level of integration and adherence to positive norms in spite of intense gossiping.

NINE
Possibilities of change in living conditions

For some time, social scientists and politicians have been involved in a debate about how to eradicate poverty. Is it society as a whole that must be changed, or is it the poor themselves, or perhaps both? Most contributors to the debate lean towards the view that either society or the poor are solely to blame. Those who blame society see the fault to be in the uneven and unfair distribution of resources: if we want to eliminate poverty, a radical political and economical transformation will have to take place. Provided that the poor are given dignified economic and material conditions, they will themselves – more or less automatically – eliminate all those other negative features that distinguish their present life, such as the lack of family unity and harmony, apathy, the inability to work for long-term goals and objectives, etc. In other words, they will create a (happy?) life for themselves, as the middle classes do.

The protagonists of the other view, however, argue that the root of the evil is in the poor themselves, or more specifically, in their 'culture'. This view seems to dominate these days, not only among academic experts on poverty, but also among liberal intellectuals and politicians in the USA. They base their argument on the works of the American anthropologist Oscar Lewis. Lewis developed the concept of the 'culture of poverty', based on intensive studies of poverty in Mexico and Puerto Rico. He compiled a list of about seventy features which he held to be typical of poor populations all over the world. I shall not discuss his list here, since it seems to depend on speculation and over-generalized conclusions, and has never been tested scientifically. Lewis, in fact, gives data which contradict his own statements. The reader who is interested is referred to Lewis 1959, 1961, and 1966, and also Valentine 1968 for a critical discussion.

Among all Lewis's generalizations, there is one in particular which is emphasized again and again by those who maintain that the poor themselves are to blame for their plight.

> 'Once it [the culture of poverty] comes into existence it tends to perpetuate itself from generation to generation because of its effect on the children. By the time slum children are age six or seven they have usually absorbed the basic values and attitudes of this subculture and are not psychologically geared to take full advantage of changing conditions or increased opportunities which may occur in their lifetime.'
>
> (Lewis 1966: xlv)

In the USA this particular passage has been used as a justification for all the kinds of 'war on poverty' programmes which aim to implant middle class virtues in poor children. The view has been that only when the poor have become conventional and respectable can they hope to escape their unhappy circumstances.

In another, less widely quoted passage, Lewis says: '... it is much more difficult to eliminate the culture of poverty than to eliminate poverty *per se*' (1966: li). At the same time he emphasizes that if we wish to improve the life of the poor we need *first* to eliminate their 'culture', not their physical, material situation, though the latter is much easier to fight.

Many people have asked themselves what could be the values and judgments that lie behind such an attitude. Valentine tries this answer:

> 'It is difficult to imagine what this might be, except a profound implicit conviction that the lifeways of the poor are inherently deserving of destruction. If it is relatively easy to do away with poverty itself, then why not do so and then let the ex-poor live as they please? Or if we believe there is a "culture of poverty" which is not good for those who live by it, then why not first tackle the more tractable problem of relieving their material deprivation and then go on to build upon their more comfortable circumstances in order to save them from those more difficult and deep-seated culture patterns? No, it is the "culture" that must go first, before the poor can be given what everybody else already possesses and many of us take for granted. In short, the poor must become "middle-class", perhaps through "psychiatric treatment", and then we shall see what can be done about their poverty.'
>
> Valentine (1968: 75)

And he adds (p. 145):

'There is certainly empirical evidence of pathology, incompetence and other kinds of inadequacy among the people of the ghettos and slums, as there is in the rest of society. There can be no doubt that living in poverty has its own destructive effect on human capacities and that these impairments become part of the whole process perpetuating deprivation. The vital questions are, how important are the internal disabilities of the lower class and how are they related to significant external factors?'

Readers who are interested in the problems and polemics regarding poverty and the culture of poverty may turn to the above-mentioned book by Valentine. It gives a comprehensive and well-balanced account of the theme with a complete bibliography.

My own view is that each concrete situation of poverty, that is, life as lived by the poor, is created through an *interplay* of circumstances both in the larger society and within the local environment of the poor. The fundamental preconditions of poverty are not created by the poor themselves, but by political and economical circumstances in society. But the concrete *shape* that poor people give to their life emerges through a multitude of small daily decisions which they themselves make. Their particular life style is not determined by nature but represents only one possibility among many. So when experts like Gans (1970:149) claim that research aiming at fighting poverty should concentrate on the analysis of the political economy of society as a whole, and ignore the actual situation of the poor, I see this as a fundamental misconception. In order to predict the *effects* of practical assistance given by society to improve the conditions of the poor, we need intensive studies of their daily life and behaviour patterns. Programmes for fighting poverty must be based on an understanding of the interplay between *all* the factors which create this unhappy life situation.

Such an understanding is best obtained by observation of situations where the living conditions of a group of poor people are changing. To my knowledge, there is as of today no material available on this for the poor in Cairo. But a few individuals and families in my study have strategies whereby they strive to improve their conditions. By analysing these attempts it is possible to discover some of the dynamics in the relation between the activities of individuals and the conditions in society.

To improve its situation, a family must have a plan or strategy to pursue in one or several of its sectors of activity. Also, it must have an internal organization which provides the degree of co-ordination and loyalty which is needed to enable it to carry out its decisions.

If we look only at the fourteen complete families in my sample, how do they stand with respect to these requirements? The preceding chapters have given ample evidence that the families generally fail fundamentally in this respect. The members are divided, and have partly different, partly conflicting objectives and interests. But two of the families have a different structure as a management unit, and therefore they are able to make decisions which are beyond the other families. The difference consists of much greater loyalty and trust between husband and wife, better ability to co-ordinate, and clearer and more articulate plans for improving their life (see p. 71). In the following section I shall refer to these two types of families as 'divided' and 'aspiring' families respectively. And I shall try to show for a series of sectors of activity what possibilities for upward social mobility are open to each of the different decision structures.

Let us first examine the families' potential for making a coherent plan for their economy: can the families increase their incomes, and can they pursue a different, more adequate strategy regarding consumption and saving to increase their welfare and/or make investment possible? In Chapter 3 I gave data of the main providers' work and income levels. We saw that the head of the family is the sole provider, that all men except one have two jobs, a main job and an extra job, and that the average working day is about ten hours long. Theoretically they could then increase their incomes in two ways: by getting a better paid main job or by investing more time and energy in the extra jobs. These possibilities, however, remain theoretical due to the considerable unemployment in Cairo – denied officially, but in all other instances estimated at a high figure. The competition for jobs means that an influential go-between (*wasṭa*) or bribes (*rashwa*) are necessary to get anywhere, both of which are beyond the reach of the poor. An idea of the lack of work opportunities in Cairo can be given by the fact that one of the two ambitious men in my material, Mustafa, has decided to go and work in Kuwait. He is only one of many men in the country who see work outside his home country as the only road to a really improved standard of living. After working for ten years in Egypt he could not expect to earn more than £14 a month in his main job – this in spite of having completed secondary education.[1]

[1] He did not leave, however, until November 1978, and then for Saudi Arabia, where he was earning a net income of £300 a month – an increase of £270 a month in relation to what he had been earning in Egypt with his secondary job too. He sent all the money home (as he had free room and board) and his wife was beaming with joy and pride as she held the money up to me and exclaimed, 'Look, £300, don't you want to

In most communities in the world, families will solve their problems by a strategy aimed at exploitation of all the members' potential to work for shared objectives. In Cairo such a strategy is out of the question because the father totally lacks any sanctions except precisely those stemming from the fact that the other family members are dependent on him as their provider. Sons cannot expect to inherit either money or a social position from him, and from the moment they no longer need the father as a provider, the membership in their family of birth is only a burden to them. Therefore, they choose to form their own independent family as early as possible.

Consequently, the critical question must be how the families can economize with their actual resources so as to create the preconditions to improve their situation. The two aspiring families in this respect differ from the divided families. In Chapter 3 I gave data on the concrete consumption patterns of the families, and showed that they are in a chronic situation of crisis with respect to covering the basic necessities. However, in most families, the whole of a man's wages are not allocated to shared family expenses: a considerable part of it goes on his personal consumption (cigarettes, cafés, and transport). Men choose to hide the actual figures – for reasons of internal family politics. For two men, however, I have managed to extract this type of information: the wealthiest man in this sample spends almost one third of his total income, £15 out of £51, on his own consumption, whereas the rest of the family of eleven, including himself, eat, dress, and live on the rest. One of the poorest men keeps a family of eight on £23 a month, taking a good fifth, £5 for his own consumption.

The providers of the two aspiring families, on the contrary, choose to spend as little as possible on themselves: they are the only

borrow some?' Her expectation is that Mustafa will continue to work in Saudi Arabia until the children are grown (i.e. about eighteen years old) and come home for only one month a year. The separation is hard on her; she writes to him every single day; but there is no other solution to her problems as she sees it. With the first month's wages she had bought a butagas stove, with the second a refrigerator, and with the third, (which was when I last saw her) she would buy a washing machine.

Other men in the sample had also become labour migrants: Ahmed had gone to Libya and Abdullah to Saudi Arabia. They had been away for a year (January 1979). However, Ahmed reportedly found work and life so trying that he was expected to return to Cairo for good at any time, despite his wife's wishes. Abdullah's wife, on the other hand, expressed concern that Abdullah was not happy and said she had written to him to say that he should return: she wanted him, not the money (she has no relatives in Cairo, and is strongly attached to her husband). Both these wives had in the past year (1978) been able to acquire a butagas stove, refrigerator, and washing machine, tape-recorder, and smart furniture.

two men who do not smoke. This sacrifice has profound implications for the family's chances of improving its status. The value is not only in the extra pennies they thus have to spend, perhaps more important are the consequences in terms of loyalty within the family: because material goods are seen by the wife as the most unequivocal expression of her husband's love for her, he *creates*, by giving her everything he has, family loyalty. As mentioned above, these two wives are the only ones, both in and outside my material, whom I have never heard criticizing their husbands; on the contrary, they express respect for, and admiration of them (see p. 71).

In the divided families, the wife sees herself as the only one who strives to plan, economize, and save, with all the odds against her: an irregular flow of money and the many unsatisfied needs in the home at any time makes saving very difficult. The women themselves see the saving club as the only possible way to save — even for amounts of only £1-£2 (the contribution may be e.g. 1p per day). But this is sometimes a way for them to lay their hands on large sums of up to £100.

The money saved is spent in two ways: on objects with consumption and prestige value or on investment. Such objects are shirts, blankets, beds, shoes, etc. The poverty and the lack in each home of a number of consumer items which are seen as necessities in Egyptian urban culture, combined with low standards and great wear and tear on almost all the items there, gives prestige to the acquisition as such of something new which can be shown off. But objects, of course, have different prestige values. Since the late sixties, a television set has ranked as the highest among the objects within reach of a family. The price varies between £100 and £150, with £50 in cash and monthly payments of £5. In 1969, only two families had television; two years later another five had it. Nothing suggests that the financial position of these families had improved in that period. But it does seem that they have seen themselves in a situation of competition: all five wives bought their television sets at the same time as their best friend. This suggests that the families can save up quite a lot for consumer goods which also interest the husband. Nevertheless, the wives in the divided families see such saving as a result of their personal efforts, not of the husband's income: when a woman was threatened by divorce, she retorted with a counter-threat: 'I shall smash up the television before I go, because that was bought by *me*!' (She could not threaten to take it with her, since she had not brought it into the marriage as part of her dowry.)

Television is seen by others as a sign that the family's most important material needs are already covered. But the flat and the family then must have an appearance confirming this. The aspiring families especially seem to attach importance to style in clothes and appearance. Therefore, they manage among other things to look well turned-out each Ramadan. Ibrahim, the one of the two aspiring husbands who has an average income, is also the only one in my sample who has managed to fulfil the cultural demands for beds for all members of the family (see p. 21). His flat is so well equipped that he has even been able to bring friends home with him (to watch the new television).

By economy and proper use of the money saved, the families can climb within their own environment, hope to leave it as a physical locality and to give their children a much better future.

The two aspiring families have already managed to raise their social status in the neighbourhood; they have been able to make contacts in circles which would otherwise be closed to them, and they avoid, definitely much more often than the divided families with the same standard of living, the subjective experience of stigma.

Plans aiming at leaving the back street environment, however, make investment necessary. My seventeen families can only see two potential ways of investing. One is a building-lot (in the country by the Pyramids) and the other is education. Two of the women in the study have about £70 invested in a building-lot, but it is doubtful whether their dream of a house of their own will ever be realized. Their husbands are not interested in the enterprise and in August 1972 both of them owed between five and eight monthly payments of £5 (the full price is about £350). I know however two families (outside the sample) who moved out to the Pyramid area in the summer of 1972 and started to build a house with their own hands. They preferred a primitive and provisional life in a shack-like house of their own for a while rather than go on 'losing' the rent of £5 a month in the back street.

Education is the other form of investment. The two types of families have remarkably different attitudes to this. In the divided families, as mentioned above, the woman's orientation to education is in dramatic contrast to the man's apparent lack of interest (see p. 69). In the aspiring families, both husband and wife are intensely oriented towards good education for their children. Ibrahim signalled this clearly when he gave this reason for buying the television: 'There are so many programmes that the children can learn from.' (All the other families with television see the appliance only as a means of entertainment.) Mustafa values education even more highly, and shows this by his indefatigable attempts to obtain higher education for himself: for three or four years he tried to go to evening classes to take A-levels in order to go on to university: 'don't care which department – what's important is to get a certificate, for Egypt has become a country of certificates.' At last however, the financial burden became too much for the family during his education, and this is when he decided to go and work in Kuwait.

It is reasonable to suggest that the markedly different priority which the parents in the divided families give to education is connected with the difference in benefits which would result for each of them if the plan were to succeed. Here the lifelong strong bond between mother and child is relevant, as opposed to the total lack of bond between father and child (see p. 73). From a successful son, a mother can expect premiums, both in the token of material goods and social status. A father, however, can only look forward to a loss of value, by losing even more of the son's respect (see p. 71). Through a well educated daughter a mother may gain access to a beautiful home and good food – since a woman's social mobility through marriage will increase with her education. The mother may even be the one to get the privilege of looking after home and grandchildren while the daughter works. A father, on the other hand, has nothing to gain. In other words, investment in children's education is to the woman investment in her own old age – whilst to the man it is an absurd waste of money.

What expenses does education involve, and for whom? All public schooling (including universities) is free. Even so, all school children in my study who have reached the point of leaving elementary school pay school fees of £9-£12 a year (on top of this are added expenses for books, private tutors, etc.) and because of such expenses some parents, as we have seen, refuse to send their children to elementary school. Why is that? Let us first take a look at the first-form pupil: before going to school he will need better clothes than for playing in the street; he needs for example shoes, school uniform, and a school-bag. His parents reckon that the expenses the first year amount to £3-£4, and that they go up each year. School fees mean the child goes to a private school because he has failed twice in his exams at the elementary school. Only one out of seventeen pupils in the sample succeeded in his second attempt and could go on to a free public high school, where he later failed. Ten out of the sixteen took their elementary exams privately, eight of them then went on to a public high school, failed the first year, spent one to two or three years at a private school, went back to a public school, failed, etc. Many of them have paid about £15 a year in expenses at the private school because they also had to pay for books, and they often have to take extra tuition with tutors at a rate of £3 a month. It is the mother who mainly or solely struggles to provide this money (see p. 69). An indication of the strength of the desire for education, and the struggle to obtain it, is the fact that the two pupils in the sample who went through high school did this after studying for sixteen and seventeen years respectively, whereas twelve years is the norm (both went on to higher education).

These conditions reflect an interplay between circumstances in the home and society which produces the worst possible learning situation for the school-children. The external factors are connected with the standard of the schools and the teaching, and are best illustrated by the reforms proclaimed by a new school law in July 1972. From now on no elementary school class should have more than forty pupils. (Sixty had been common.) It is prohibited for the teacher to eat or knit during classes. The pupils should be examined at the end of each school-year (not after six years as before). It is not unusual for pupils from the neighbourhood to be unable to write after six years in elementary school.

The home environment makes studying even more difficult: the children have to do their homework in the room where many other or all other activities are carried out at the same time, often in deafening noise with a minimum of technical aids (four notebooks instead of ten as has been mentioned above). Under such conditions it is really quite surprising that anyone manages to take A-levels.

When education is successful, it is a splendid investment: the only person in the sample who has managed to obtain higher education, (a four-year course in a technical college) started out as a teacher with a basic salary of £17 (the labour market is so over-full that most academics must take jobs which have nothing to do with their formal competence). With overtime he earns £25 per month at the age of twenty-seven and his basic salary is raised by £1 per year. In comparison, a clerk with O-levels, publicly employed, earns only £7 a month, and has a rise of only 75p per year.

In accordance with Arab socialist ideology, the Egyptian government seems to have created the formal preconditions for mobility through education. It has established free education at all levels, fines for keeping children away from the elementary school, and a pay system *strongly* favouring education. This orientation also coincides with the individual's own views on education as the one way to social mobility.

But why then do such facilities so rarely open up a successful way out of poverty? The answer must lie in the interaction between conditions in the home and in the rest of society, which structure the actual situations and choices of the individual. What prevails is an unhappy combination of the form and quality of teaching on the one hand and a conflict-ridden home environment on the other, which largely precludes a successful result.

Another important field where public attempts actively to combat poverty have become tragically ineffective, is the population policy. The burden of providing for a large family will keep people with low incomes in poverty. Poor Egyptians themselves realize this and see family planning as a desirable and adequate objective. Married couples are free to make such decisions, since they have a mutual interest in this, and are not hampered by taboos or embarrassment. The ideal is two to three children, with both sexes represented. From official sources the family is subjected to propaganda for families with two children. It reaches them most effectively in the shape of a television commercial showing two happy, well-dressed children, brother and sister, hand in hand on their way to school. The explicit message is: 'Have two children and you'll be able to give them a good life!' But it seems that at the same time the viewers have their own idea confirmed: a family should contain children of both sexes and from that point of view the campaign for two children is badly planned.

Although there has been a great official effort to introduce effective family planning, and although the population itself has clearly formulated plans for limiting the number of children they have, I can record only a minimum of success in this sphere. In December 1969 all my fourteen complete families swore that they had had their last baby, and this statement was made so firmly that I was convinced they would succeed. But by August 1972 only two (of the thirteen remaining marriages) had *not* failed: eight of them had had one child, and one of these women feared she was pregnant once more, another two were pregnant, and the eleventh had miscarried a couple of times. What is the explanation of this discrepancy? Was the plan only empty words or are other circumstances to blame for their failure in carrying it out?

There is nothing to suggest that their wishes to limit their families were only empty words, and several married couples gave vivid descriptions of fits of hysterics when the pregnancy was confirmed. Most of them sought illegal abortion through a doctor (abortion injections at £1.00 each), home-brewed herb medicine, and mechanical attempts to abort by hitting the stomach, jumping down the stairs, etc. The explanation therefore must be in deficient contraceptive devices or ineffective methods. The most popular method is the pill, which eleven out of the thirteen women use. They obtain it from public clinics where it is made available for 5p per pack, whereas the standard price is 20p. But this programme fails for a number of reasons:

(1) Sometimes the clinic claims to have run out of pills. Rather than pay the higher price, which equals food for the whole family for one day, the women will then take a risk.

(2) Information and understanding are defective: some women take the pill only every other day (so as not to become weak or ill) or only on nights when they sleep with their husbands; or they know that they should take it for three weeks and then rest for one week but do not know which week, etc.

(3) Mistrust of anything subsidized or provided by the Government: folk wisdom proclaims that the 5p pill has a number of dangerous side effects: giddiness, loss of hair, loss of weight, fatigue, pains in the chest, etc. People believe that the cheap pill, as opposed to the 20p pill from the chemist, does not contain vitamins (*vitamināt*). To compensate for this, the 5p pill must be taken with nutritious food (*çeza* – that is high protein food) which they simply cannot afford. These views are so deeply rooted that they cannot be shaken: every imaginable illness is blamed on the 5p pill.

(4) Private practitioners seem to oppose the programme according to my informants by advising patients to give up the pill for a month as a cure for various illnesses.

The coil is another method which can be had from the public clinic. But the information that it can be fitted for the low cost of 10p had only reached three of the women in the study. Most of them seem to think that it costs several pounds. Moreover, terror stories about it flourish (it causes abortions, destroys the male organ, etc.). The fact that a male doctor fits it at the public clinic is also a contributory factor in the women's reluctance to accept the offer. Only two of the women in the study have tried the coil, and only one successfully.

The result of this failure in family planning can be seen in *Table 9(1)*.

In other words, there is no clear evidence that the birth rate has gone down in the present generation. In spite of significantly more accessible and effective contraceptive methods, the tragic conclusion is that it is not unlikely that complete families of six to seven children can be expected.

Table 9(1): *Birth rates*

	married years	living children	dead children
non-aspiring families	27	9	3
	25	7	1
	24	6	2
	23	7	1
	18	6	2
	10	5	2
	10	2	(several abortions)
	9	4	
	8	4	
	7	3	
	5	4	
aspiring families	7	3	
	6	2	

Only the two aspiring families show a pattern which may imply that they will succeed in controlling the size of their family. Mustafa, who tried to secure a higher education, had only one child until he decided to emigrate after five years. Ibrahim's children now amount to three after violent arguments between him and his wife: he wanted a son as well as the two daughters whereas she refused to have any more children. Once he had had a son, however, both he and his wife agreed that the family was complete, and because of the usual view that the pill has problems and dangers attached to it, the wife immediately had a coil fitted.[1]

In addition to the financial burden which natural growth imposes on the provider, he may also be burdened in a way he cannot control at all: the laws of the nation make him financially responsible for a disabled father, unsupported mother, sister, or half-sister on his father's side, a dead brother's children, etc. This can have quite absurd results: a retired man remarried at the age of sixty-five and in the following years had four children. He expected his adult son to come to their financial support. The son, who was providing for his own family of five members with an income of £10 a month, categorically refused. The father then took him to court

[1]However, before April 1975 both these mothers had had another baby each, because, they said, the women could not continue with the pill or the coil, for health reasons. Two years later Mustafa's wife had yet another child.

and the son was ordered by the court to pay his father £2.50 per month. Now the father is dead: the widow works and so contributes to the support of the four children. But once she remarries, as is expected, the complete financial responsibility for the children will fall on their half-brother.

In 1972 another two of the fourteen men in the study had similar extra financial burdens: one provided for his imprisoned brother's children and one for his dead brother's children. Two of the three female heads of families in the material were provided for in a similar manner by sons and brothers/half-brothers.

The inefficient bureaucracy creates further burdens. A divorced woman has to go to court to get her rightful alimony. Court cases cost money and it can easily take a year before the court order is issued and the documents pass through official red tape. Meanwhile someone has to support her (and possibly small children) and the brother is then the closest. For example, the same unfortunate man who had to provide for his four half-brothers and sisters in 1972 also had to support a divorced older sister with two children. His constant, desperate exclamation is: 'From the day father died I only wish Allah would take me back too.'

When a family is hit by illness, it can create financial burdens of serious dimensions. An able-bodied man soon loses his badly needed extra income. If his main job is in the private sector, he will also lose part of his main income. The same thing may happen to public employees although state-owned companies give sick leave with pay for up to one month per year. But in order to get paid while off sick, a man must obtain a certificate from one of the doctors employed by the company's health department. It is not easy for a poor man to get that certificate. However sick he is, he has to go to the health department, often several times, in the hope of finding the right person. Besides, the certificate costs bribes. One man I know had to pay £2 for such a certificate and still did not receive it. In other words, he lost both the bribe and a whole month's pay.

As mentioned above, patients will try to avoid buying medicines. They are *very* expensive (in academic circles people maintain that this is because doctors are paid commission on the medicines they prescribe and will therefore choose the most expensive ones). But in more serious cases, where the patient realizes that expensive medicines are absolutely necessary, the usual pattern is to sell belongings, sometimes nearly all one's furniture. Consequently, most ways to mobility by financial success are closed to most individuals and households. Moreover, people themselves see their situation as much worse now than it was in 1950 ('since the days of the English and King Farouk'). Only one of the men in my material had a good word to say about the present government and regime. (These and the following data are from 1969-70.) For all the others it stands for oppression (*zolm*), chaos (*mafísh nizám xális*), bribes (*rashwa*), exploitation of the poor, and a much reduced standard of living. The most powerful proof of these realities they see in the military defeat by Israel: 'They are two million people and we are thirty-four million plus the rest of the Arab world. And *they* won – because of the exploitation and lack of co-operation among us.'[1] On the other hand: 'In the days of the English there was system and order in this country, in those days the streets were lit and people were happy. Now people are so worn and weighed down by worries they can't see where they are going and so they keep bumping into each other. So now the world is all quarrels and anger, sadness' (*Zaçl*).

I have mentioned that no political activism aimed at improving the position of the poor in society is found in Cairo these days. But with discontent as strong as it is, are there no channels through which it is expressed? I shall try to show how such activities are blocked both inside the existing structure of society and in more revolutionary types of movement.

Let me begin with the established structure. Since 1956 Egypt has had a progressive one-party system based on the Arab Socialist Union (ASU). The people elect representatives, and the party has offices in all of Cairo's districts, where the inhabitants should be able to go with their complaints and questions.

The poor see this organization as 'ink on paper' (*ḥibra çála ilwaraq*), 'empty words' (*kalám fáçiq*), 'not in reality, but a lie' (*mish fil haqíqa – kizb!*), 'the people have no say' (*innás malhumsh kilma*). 'The representatives cannot claim anything on behalf of the poor' (*ilmanáwib mish biyiqdaru yutlubu ḥága çashan il-çalába*) because the government immediately removes anyone who disagrees with it' (*çashan illi biyitkallim didd ilḥukúma, humma biyshilúh*). 'If I go to a representative and tell him I want something, he'll say: "By your conscience, do you want them to sack me?"' (*Law ruḥt liwáḥid wa qultilu ana çáyiz ḥaga, kan yiqulli! Bi zimmitak, çayzinhum yisaqqinúni?*) Because a representative makes about £70-£80 a month, poor people find this attitude perfectly understandable.

If the ASU does not fulfil its formal functions, it has, according to some of the men, another important function – for the

[1] Following the victory in the October War these attitudes have changed.

President. 'It has been created for him especially – as an organ of acclaim! Can't you see on television all those sitting there listening while *he* speaks and applauding every word he says? *They* are the members of the ASU and the Parliament. Their one important job is to attend his speeches and applaud them. Out of fear they applaud every single word.'

The lack of identification with the nation is shown in one man's choice to give the following event as an example of these conditions:

'Once, in a speech, Nasser suggested that all public employees should give two days' wages to the war with Israel. The parliament applauded deafeningly instead of standing up to fight against this suggestion. That is *oppression*. We low-paid public employees were on the verge of tears when pay day came and we found two days' pay deducted from our wages.'

Local ASU representatives, however, also control certain public facilities such as jobs and flats. It is characteristic that the representatives do not exploit these to get political clients for themselves, but only for material gain. A poor woman who went to the ASU office and asked them to help her with accommodation because her shack on the roof was to be demolished was asked for a bribe of £20. This act is in accordance with the folk generalization that 'people sell their conscience for money' (see p. 49) and shows how poor people are devoid of political influence through regular channels. The poor are useless as clients to local politicians, who again are powerless in higher levels of political organization.

There does not seem to be any real alternative, in the form of collective political action among the poor. Such organization is impeded by the ubiquitous mistrust and suspicion which are indeed so strong that Cairo does not even have organized crime. Suspicion takes two forms. People are afraid of informers: if a potential leader tries to mobilize support, all experience will tell him that the people he appeals to will most probably try to obtain immediate gain for themselves by reporting against him. They on their side will mistrust his intentions and be afraid that this might be a provocation to take away from them what little they have. They are all afraid of losing their jobs, since they rightly or wrongly believe that every superior has complete power, and that rights in a job can only be protected by submission. Moreover, mistrust undermines their faith in long-range objectives: if a move is successful, the leaders will reap the fruits but the small people will get nothing. As an example they point to Nasser's treatment of his co-revolutionaries: all twenty-four were dismissed.

Possibilities of change in living conditions 163

On the whole, these poor people have an overwhelming experience of being the victims of an unfair, oppressive social system. Most of them consider themselves powerless to improve their own situation and have in the best of cases only a hope for their children, that they might escape the stigma of poverty through a better education. If the adults' situation is to be improved, *the system must be changed*, as they see it. Egypt must get a strong and effective administration which genuinely serves the interests of the poor, and a bureaucracy working on an objective basis, fairly and justly. The system should reward co-operation (*taçáwun*), conscientious work (*shuçl bi zimma*), and order/organization (*nizám*). There is no doubt among the poor that the lack of these three virtues is the root of all social evil in Egypt these days (1972).

For if there were co-operation, then the rich would be willing to share with the poor and those better off would help those worse off. If conscientious work was done generally, then the bureaucrats, doctors, medical staff, tailors, shoemakers, etc. would all do the responsible, high-quality work they are obliged to do. With organization in the country, even a poor man would be protected and secure, not like now at the mercy of other people's highhandedness, irresponsibility and enmity, but would be able to plan his life.

None of the poor I know have any hope that radical reforms of this kind will take place in Egypt in the foreseeable future. The main barrier, as they see it, is Egyptian national character. Everyone is only seeking his own advantage. The desire for ever more and better consumer goods seems insatiable. Only a government which forcibly took from the rich and gave to the poor would mean a true salvation.

We have, however, seen also that Egypt's present regime (1972) has instituted measures greatly to the benefit of those poor who do take advantage of them, such as education and family planning. But we have also noted that the birth control programme fails, partly due to the negative attitudes of the poor themselves, such as their mistrust of the cheap pill. Going back to the introductory part of this chapter, is it logical to ask whether Cairo's population has a 'culture', a 'culture of poverty' which blocks or reduces their ability to take advantage of real, positive measures on the part of society to help them?

First we must clarify what is meant by the word 'culture'. The concept has been used in many different ways by social scientists, and much confusion has ensued, not least in the discussion of poverty. Oscar Lewis, for example, uses a concept of culture which includes the patterns of people's actual behaviour as well as their attitudes and values, in other words, for him it embraces both the results of actions and the conditions for action. By definition, then, all behaviour patterns among the poor which are different from those of the middle-classes are seen as features of a distinctive, deviant culture, i.e. a 'culture of poverty'. And because the middle-classes tend to see the behaviour of the poor as something inferior and contemptible, it is natural to conclude with Lewis that the first step in eliminating poverty is to eradicate the 'culture of poverty'.

My own view is that such a concept of culture confuses rather than explains. Against it I shall pose a definition of culture which embraces only values, norms, and forms of understanding; that is, what standards and knowledge people have learned, and which of these they use to interpret their world and their own actions – but not including the concrete choices they make and the actions they carry out. This will enable us to differentiate between cause and effect; between the conditions for an action and the behaviour resulting from such conditions. And 'culture' becomes only one set of conditions; another being the factors in people's physical and social environments which constrain their freedom to act. Such situation-bound factors are their material resources, their physical environment, and the interests and sanctions of those with whom they interact. With such a concept of culture we will also be able to *test* the question of whether the poor have their own culture. If we can show that the poor people's behaviour patterns can be explained in terms of their scarce resources and environmental situation, we do not need to construct any special culture for them. This has provided the basis for my analysis of much of the previous data. I have identified behaviour patterns among the poor in Cairo which are different from those practised by higher classes, for example the woman's very dominant position in the home and the children's lack of respect for their father. But I have been able to explain these without postulating any other values for poor women and children than for those who are better off. I have explained the patterns as *solutions* which the poor, in their especially deprived situation, have arrived at in their attempt to realize values which they share with urban Egyptians in general. If my analysis is correct we can also claim that given the middle classes' resources and starting-point, the poor would probably have behaved just like them, whereas Egyptian middle-class people exposed to the situation of the poor very likely would adjust as they do.

The conclusion is that in my material I do not find any evidence that the poor people of Cairo maintain their poverty because of deficiencies within their own culture. I find no evidence that these seventeen families have a 'culture of poverty' which differs from Egyptian urban culture generally. It is, however, possible that this conclusion is based on too fragile a foundation: my knowledge of life among the Egyptian upper and middle classes is too limited, and there is therefore a danger that I may overlook some cultural differences. Also, my understanding of poor men and their world is too shallow, and it is possible that they have specific values which I do not know. As mentioned above, I only have first-hand data about their activities at home, and this is but one sector of their life.

On the basis of my understanding of life among poor people in Cairo, my hypothesis is, however, that they do not have a culture of poverty which obstructs the improvement of their conditions. Their scepticism about welfare measures is not exclusive to them. The mistrust of the cheap pill, for example, I believe is shared by Egyptians of higher status. High as well as low have the idea that the more expensive an object or a service, the better it is, plus a deeply rooted mistrust of subsidized goods and services from the government. And who knows? Perhaps the cheap pill *is* inferior.

Other features of the 'culture of poverty' which have been mentioned as characteristic are apathy and inability to renounce present consumption in favour of long-range objectives and investment in the future. Where poor people in Cairo are concerned, I cannot find these features. On the contrary it is remarkable what eagerness and will to sacrifice women and children display in order to invest in education. I find no support for Lewis's generalization that slum children, when they reach the age of six or seven, are no longer psychologically equipped to take advantage of increased opportunities. The fact that the men on their side are negatively disposed I have explained from simple utility theory: the way families work, it would not be in *their* interest to invest. Thus it is not a question of apathy but a simple failure of family loyalty. Poverty certainly lies behind it, but not a *'culture* of poverty'. My data and my impressions from the back streets in general suggest that the material conditions are decisive: if a married couple have a material starting-point above a certain level, they will develop stronger loyalty and solidarity. Provided my analysis of self-realization (Chapter 8) and the formation of roles in marriage (Chapter 7) is right, the explanation is to be found in the self-respect and social status the both parties derive from a presentable home, which then becomes an incentive for them to co-operate to maintain and improve their status and protect their shared honour.

When the poor people in Cairo maintain that they themselves have no opportunity really to improve their situation, but that assistance must come from outside, I agree with them on the whole. My slight reservation would be that most families could improve their conditions somewhat if the men chose to spend less money on their personal expenses. But then in a sense I presuppose that they should live according to values which are contrary to the Egyptian male ideal of indulgence and independence. I do not agree with the women's criticism of the men: that they could and should work harder. The load of work which men have already assumed seems to me much too heavy, and this is often reflected in thin bodies and worn faces. Neither do I agree with the men's criticism that the women squander money. On the whole the women seem to economize in a painstaking and even obsessional fashion.

Large-scale assistance on the part of society is necessary if the several millions of poor people in Cairo are to experience a real improvement in their conditions. Any counter-suggestions to the effect that the poor must first help themselves by ridding themselves of their 'culture of poverty' are based on unproved postulates, and serve as an excuse for the authorities. It is the external economic and political conditions that are at the root of the poor people's handicap. Meanwhile I maintain my assertion that life as lived by the poor in the back streets is not a simple consequence of external conditions alone, but emerges in *conjunction* with local conditions. My whole analysis in these chapters has aimed precisely at showing how the poor people's reactions to such external conditions are specific *solutions* chosen by the individual on the basis of his or her understanding and aspirations, values and needs. Thus the poor do create *their own life* and *their own environment* in a real sense – not because they have a 'deviant' subculture which makes them poor, but simply because they have a culture on the whole like that of other urban Egyptians, and it guides their reactions and choices in the unhappy situation in which they find themselves. The gossip and people's talk which destroy so much, for example, arise not only because people live very close together and have few possessions, but because poor Egyptians have certain Egyptian views on the importance of material goods, and so find solutions to their need to 'think well of themselves' in terms of this. Rich Egyptians with greater resources can practise other solutions, so people's talk probably flourishes less among them. But people with a different culture – and therefore different views of what is needed to think well of themselves – would make quite different choices and create quite different social environments than the poor in Cairo have done, even under identical external circumstances.

Measures to improve the poor people's living conditions can thus be based neither on the idea that we face a definite 'culture of poverty' which has to be eliminated, nor that we can improve the quality of life by concentrating on external conditions. They must be based on an understanding of the *interplay* between external and local conditions. They must provide the individual with real options which he himself can see are advantageous in terms of what he wishes to achieve in life; and they must be designed so that the individual will adopt solutions which will also have a positive effect on society as a whole, in order that one man's success will not spell the other man's failure. Programmes for action which are designed from a simpler model of causal connections than I here propose will not achieve their targets, but might even aggravate rather than improve the life of the poor.

Appendix – prices

Illness: Medical consultation costs a minimum of 15p but this amount is a trifle compared to the price of medicines. In a hospital close by there is in fact the possibility of a consultation for only 5p and free medicines, but the patients do not trust the doctor to bother to make the proper diagnosis. And they seldom use the free medicines because the man behind the counter will say they are not available at the moment – they suspect he sells the medicines and puts the profit into his own pocket. As a consequence, poor people see a doctor only in an emergency.

School: Uniform, shoes, and schoolbag for the first form cost about £3.50. Private school fees are about £9-£12 a year, excluding schoolbooks and clothes.

Ramadan and Beiram are the two big celebrations and bring large expenses for food, festive clothes, and presents. Festive clothes for a seven-year-old boy for example, trousers, sweater, shoes and socks alone will cost about £6.

Men's clothes: Trousers, shirt, shoes, and socks for daily wear at work cost about £7 for a quality which wears out quickly. A sweater, a necessary garment in winter, is about £5.

Women's clothes: A nightdress-like garment to wear about the house in summer is about 70p cash, 90p on hire purchase. A similar dress of wool for wear in winter is about £1.40, shoes about £2, a summer dress £2-£3, a winter woollen dress £3.50-£4.

Children's clothes: Summer pyjamas for a seven-year-old: about 80p, winter pyjamas £1.20, vest 20p, canvas shoes 60p (lasts for a maximum of a couple of months) ordinary shoes £1.50, knee-socks 20p.

Towel about 50p cash, 70-80p on hire purchase, sheets £1.50 cash, woollen rug £3.50, or £4.50 on hire purchase, a cotton blanket for a double bed about £4.50, a double bed £10-£18, a large clothes cupboard (none of the flats have any fitted cupboards) £20-£40.

Bibliography

AbuLughod, J. (1972) *Cairo – One Thousand-One Years of the City Victorious.* Princeton University Press.
Ammar, H. (1954) *Growing Up in an Egyptian Village.* Octagon.
Berger, M. (1964) *The Arab World Today.* New York: Anchor Books.
Dickson, H.R.P. (1052) *The Arab of The Desert* London: George Allen & Unwin.
Gans, H.J. (1970) 'Poverty and Culture'. In Townsend (1970) *The Concept of Poverty*
Goffman, E. (1959) *The Presentation of Self in Everyday Life* London: Doubleday.
Hannerz, U. (1971) *The Study of Afro-American Cultural Dynamics* In Southwestern Journal of Anthropology 27: 2, Summer.
Lewis, O. (1959) *Five Families: Mexican Case Studies in the culture of poverty.* New York: Basic Books.
Lewis, O. (1961)*The Children of Sanchez.* New York: Random House.
Lewis, O. (1966) *La Vida: A Puerto Rican family in the Culture of Poverty.* New York: Random House.
Musil, A. (1928) *Manners and Customs of the Rwala Bedouins.* American Geographical Society: Oriental Explorations and Studies No. 6. New York: Crane.
Peristiani, J.G. (1965) *Honour and Shame: The Values of Mediterranean Society.* Chicago: University of Chicago Press.
Rein, M. (1970) Problems in the Definition and Measurement of Poverty. In Townsend (1970) *The Concept of Poverty.*
Schorr, A.L. (1970) Housing Policy and Poverty. In Townsend (1970) *The Concept of Poverty.*
Townsend, P. (1970) Measures and Explanations of Poverty in

High Income and Low Income Countries. In Townsend (1970) *The Concept of Poverty*. New York: Elsevier

Valentine, C.A. (1968) *Culture and Poverty. Critique and Counter-Proposals*. Chicago: University of Chicago Press.

Index

Abdullah: lied to, 142-3; as mediator, 52-5
Abu-Lughod, J., 17
accommodation, 19-23
acquaintances, 60, 62
Ahmed, his friendship with Abdullah, 54
alliances, 105, 110-11, 126
Amin and Umm Gamal, 115-20
Amina, and her father, 143-4
Ammar, H., 2, 65, 66n., 72n., 85, 124n.
apathy, 165
Arab Socialist Union, the, 161-3
arenas
  men's, 49-55, 101
  women's, 55-60
aspiring families, 151, 152-4, 159
authority dramatization, 103, 108

'backstage', 24, 55, 125
back streets, the, 18-19
bed-space, 21-2
Berger, M., 2-3, 124n.
birth rates, 159
borrowing money, see under money
bribes, 135, 151
bride-price, 84-5, 93

cafés, 50-51
charity, 12-14
children
  and education, 69, 154-6
  effect of, on marriage, 110-22
  and family conflicts, 67-8, 104
  and parents, 64-9
  and play, 66

children, cont.,
  and visits, 57
Christians, 6, 16, 47
city, the, 25
clothes,
  cost of, 168 app.
  distribution of, 12-14
confirmatory circles, 138-41
confrontations, 131-2
contraceptives, see family planning
conversion, 132, 134
corporations, 41, 73
courtship, see under marriage
cultural ideals, 43, 124-5
culture, concepts of, 163-4
'culture of poverty', the, 148, 164-5

dependants, 159-60
Dickson, H.R.P., 141
diet, 33-4
divided families, 151, 153
divorce, 103, 105-6, 108
door-sitting, 19, 23
dowry, 85, 93-4

education, 69, 154-6
Eliot, T.S., 123
emotions, 9
employment
  opportunities, 151
  of men, 29, 31-2
  of women, 37, 43
enemies, 61-3, 138

families, the
  location of, 10 fig., 16
  roles and relationships in, 41-3

family budgets, 28-40
fmily conflicts, 67-8, 104
family networks, 8 fig., 16
family planning, 36, 157-8
father-child relationships, 65, 68, 69-71
father, loss of, 75-6
father-son relationships, 71
flats, 20-1, 22
folk generalizations, 47-8, 56
'folk neighbourhood', 17, 23
'French neighbourhood', 17
friendship
  and alliance, 126
  between men, 50, 51
  between women, 56-60
  with author, 5-7, 14

Gamal, and the sweater, 76-80
Gans, H.J., 150
gender roles, 43-7
generalizations, *see* folk generalizations
gifts, 132-3
Goffman, E., 25n.
gossip, 58, 94, 130-1
Growing Up in an Egyptian Village 2

Hamdi, and the sweater, 77-80
Hannerz, U., 23
Hassan, and Umm Ali, 2
hospitality, 37, 51, 59, 134-5
house ownership, 19-20
hygiene, 4-5

Ibrahim, and his children, 70-1, 154, 159
ideology of honour, 141-2
illness, 160, 168 app.
incomes, 28-40, 151
information control, 49, 144-5, 146
in-laws, 60-1, 108-9, 110, 112-13
inter-family conflicts, 51-2
interplay of external and local conditions, 150, 167
investment, 154

jobs, *see* employment
justice, concepts of, 14

Laila
  and: conversion, 134; Gamal's sweater, 77-80; the needlework,

Laila, *cont.*,
  140; Mahmoud, 86-91
Lewis, O., 148-9, 164-5
Liebow, E, ix

Mahmoud, his courtship of Laila, 86-90
male relatives, 113
marriage
  concept of, 81-2
  and courtship, 82-4
  and conflict, 52, 85
  husband's expectations of, 100
  and kin groups, 93
  and sanctions, 103-4, 106-7
  wife's expectations of, 100
  and wife's forms of values, 105
  see also Laila and Mahmoud; Mona and Abdu
material goods, 127-8, 133-7
middle classes, the, 164
mistrust, 59, 126
mobility, 23-5
Mona and Abdu, 91-2
money
  and borrowing, 35, 102, 110, 128
  the problem of, 120
moral sanctions, 46-7
moral values, 137
Moslems, 47-8
mother-child relationships, 65-9, 72-4
mother, loss of, 74
Musil, A., 141
Mustafa
  and: children's education, 70-1, 155; employment, 151; family planning, 159; relationship with father, 139
myth creation, 143

naming customs, 73
national identity, 28
networks, among women, 60-3
newly married women, 108-9
note-taking, 12

Omanis, 9
overcrowding, 20-1

participant observation, 1, 4, 7, 9, 12
'people's talk', 144
Peristiani, J.G., 141
political alternatives, 162-3

Index

population policy, 157
poverty
  definitions of, 26-8
  eradication of, 148-9
  see also 'culture of poverty'
  Presentation of Self in Everyday Life, The, 25n.
prices, 168 app.

Ramadan, 35, 37, 76, 132
recognition
  and comparison with others, 128-9
  and confrontations, 131-2
  and folk generalizations, 55-6
  and gossip, 130-1
  and ideals, 124
  and material goods, 127-8, 135
  and relationships, 125-7
  and self-praise, 131
  and versions of events, 129-30
Rein, M., 26
relatives
  of the man, 52, 60, see also in-laws and the newly married, 108
  of the woman, 60, 72-3, 104-5, 113
  see also siblings; sisters; stepmothers
religion, 16, 47
resources, control of, 133
role solutions, of married women, 107-22

saving clubs, 36, 153
scapegoats, in marriage, 100
self-confirmation, 125
self-presentation, concept of, 44, 58
self-realization, 123, 124
Shorr, A., 20, 26
sibling relationships, 72, 76-80
sisters, 71-2
Soad, and the photograph, 143
social anthropology, 1
social interaction, 47-9
social recognition, *see* recognition
stepmothers, 74-5

Tally's Corner, ix
teenage children, 115-22
television sets, 143

Umm Aleyya, and criticism of others, 141
Umm Ali
  and: the author, 2, 3-4;
  the butane gas, 145;
  the cakes, 57-8;

Umm Ali, *cont*.,
  employment, 121;
  Hassan, 99-100;
  the Koran reading, 129-30;
  her nephew, 142;
  the Pepsi Cola, 134;
  social relations, 61-3;
  Umm Foad, 57-8, 140-1;
  Umm Mohammed, 111, 112
Umm Anwar, and the cakes, 133
Umm Foad
  and: her brother, 128;
  the fish, 127-8;
  the housekeeping money, 120;
  moral criticism, 137-8;
  the neighbour, 131;
  Umm Ali, 57-8, 140-1
Umm Gamal
  and: accusations of flirting, 145;
  Amin, 115-20;
  criticism of others, 142;
  the new dress, 140;
  her sister, 131;
  Umm Aleyya, 139;
  Zenab, 57
Umm Hamada, and the cooking, 145
Umm Hussein
  and: Abdullah, 111-12;
  the clothes, 142;
  enmity, 138;
  Gamila, 144;
  in-laws, 113-14;
  the soap, 140;
  social conversion, 134;
  social relations, 61-3;
  Umm Mohammed, 52-5, 132
Umm Mohammed
  and: Ahmed, 96-8, 111-13;
  enmity, 138;
  in-laws, 128-9;
  Karima, 140;
  social relations, 61-2;
  Um Hussein, 52-5, 132;
  visit to the country, 144;
  visit to her father, 74
Umm Said, and information control, 145
Umm Sami, and 'people's talk', 145
unknown women, 61
USA, the, ix, 148-9

Valentine, C.A., 148, 149-50
violence, 133

Walter, 28
widows, 75